KU-676-017

GERMANY
in Pictures

Jeffrey Zuehlke

Lerner Publications Company

Contents

Lerner Publishing Group realizes that current information and statistics quickly become out of date. To extend the usefulness of the Visual Geography Series, we developed www.vgsbooks.com, a website offering links to up-to-date information, as well as in-depth material, on a wide variety of subjects. All of the websites listed on www.vgsbooks.com have been carefully selected by researchers at Lerner Publishing Group. However, Lerner Publishing Group is not responsible for the accuracy or suitability of the material on any website other than <www.lernerbooks.com>. It is recommended that students using the Internet be supervised by a parent or teacher. Links on www.vgsbooks.com will be regularly reviewed and updated as needed.

Website address: www.lernerbooks.com

Lerner Publications Company
A division of Lerner Publishing Group
241 First Avenue North
Minneapolis, MN 55401 U.S.A.

web enhanced @ www.vgsbooks.com

CULTURAL LIFE   46

► Religion. Literature, Film, and Television. Architecture, Art, and Music. Festivals and Food. Sports and Recreation.

THE ECONOMY   56

► Manufacturing and Trade. Agriculture, Fishing, and Forestry. Mining and Energy. Transportation and Tourism. The Future.

FOR MORE INFORMATION

Library of Congress Cataloging-in-Publication Data

Zuehlke, Jeffrey, 1968–
    Germany in pictures / by Jeffrey Zuehlke.— Rev. and updated ed.
       p.   cm. — (Visual geography series)
    Includes bibliographical references and index.
    ISBN: 0-8225-4681-7 (lib. bdg. : alk. paper)
    1. Germany—Juvenile literature. 2. Germany—Pictorial works—Juvenile literature. I. Title. II. Visual
geography series (Minneapolis, Minn.)
DD17 .Z84 2003
943—dc21   2002009442

Manufactured in the United States of America
1 2 3 4 5 6 - JR - 08 07 06 05 04 03

INTRODUCTION

On October 3, 1990, East Germany and West Germany, separated since the end of World War II (1939–1945), became a single, united nation. Reunification made Germany Europe's second largest country (after Russia) and the continent's largest economic power. Millions of Germans rejoiced at reunification and looked forward to a new era of German prosperity.

But a united Germany has been the exception rather than the norm in the country's long history. Germany's dense forests and river valleys were first settled by nomads about one hundred thousand years ago. In the late eighth century A.D., the emperor Charlemagne united these groups under his rule. After Charlemagne's death, local barons and dukes established semi-independent principalities (realms of princes) in the eastern part of the empire.

These realms later became a part of the Holy Roman Empire, a confederation of states in central Europe and northern Italy. For centuries all the Holy Roman emperors came from the Habsburg family—a

web enhanced @ www.vgsbooks.com

wealthy, ethnically German dynasty (family of rulers). Yet Germany itself remained a patchwork of semi-independent cities and states with their own rulers, laws, and customs. In the early 1800s, as the armies of the French emperor Napoleon Bonaparte entered Germany, the Holy Roman Empire collapsed.

Otto von Bismarck, a strong-willed politician from Prussia (northern Germany), united the German states into a new empire in the late 1800s. The German Empire developed its industries and built factories, shops, and a modern transportation system. Germany also used much of its growing wealth to strengthen its armed forces.

Seeking to increase its power in Europe, Germany fought two world wars in the 1900s. The first, World War I (1914–1918), ended in bitter defeat. The country's leaders were forced to sign a humiliating peace agreement that required Germany to pay billions in reparations (war damages). As a result, the economy collapsed. Millions of impoverished Germans, bitter over the harsh treatment at the hands of their

victorious neighbors, turned to Adolf Hitler and his Nazi Party for leadership in the 1930s.

Hitler restored Germany's economy and national pride but soon led the nation into a brutal war of expansion. After nearly conquering all of Europe in the first years of World War II, Germany's advances were stalled. Counterattacks by Allied armies of the United States, Britain, the Soviet Union, and others defeated Germany, devastating the country. Seeking to avoid another German threat, Allied armies occupied Germany. The Allies divided the nation and its capital, Berlin, into western and eastern zones. West Germany established a democratic government. In East Germany, a Communist regime seized most private property and began a system of central economic planning. The two ideologies created two German cultures that existed side by side from the late 1940s to the late 1980s. While West Germans enjoyed a remarkable economic recovery and one of the highest standards of living in the world, East Germany struggled under strict Communist rule.

Reunification came about in 1990, after the collapse of Communist rule in Eastern Europe. Since then, a capitalist economic system has been in place throughout Germany. Billions of dollars have been transferred from the prosperous West to the developing "new states" of the East. New buildings, homes, and roads have been built in the new states. The arts and other forms of expression flourish openly once more.

But the transition to a united Germany has not always been smooth. German leaders predicted that it would take a decade for the new states to become the economic equals of the Western states. Yet more than a decade has passed since reunification, and the new states continue to lag behind economically. Low wages and high unemployment rates remain serious issues, along with racial tensions. Another decade or more may be needed before the Eastern states no longer need financial support from the West.

Following the September 11, 2001 terrorist attacks on the United States, German law enforcement agencies have worked closely with U.S. agencies to track down terrorist cells within Germany. (The attacks are blamed on the terrorist group al-Qaeda. Several al-Qaeda operatives had once made their homes in Germany.) In late 2001, military action by the United States in Afghanistan destroyed al-Qaeda camps and the Taliban regime that sheltered them. In 2002 and 2003, German troops served as peacekeepers in Afghanistan. As one of the leaders of the European Union (EU), an organization of European countries, Germany has helped to shape the EU's foreign and domestic policies. These policies include Germany's acceptance of the euro, the new European currency. By embracing the euro and assisting in worldwide affairs, Germany has become an important member of the international community.

THE LAND

Germany's landscape includes flat plains, rolling hills, wide river valleys, sandy coasts, and rugged mountain ranges. Once covered by an immense forest, the nation has cut down most of its woodlands to provide land for cities, industrial zones, and farms. With a total land area of 137,846 square miles (357,019 square kilometers), Germany is slightly smaller than the state of Montana.

Germany shares borders with Denmark in the north and with Austria and Switzerland in the south. To the west of Germany are the Netherlands, Belgium, Luxembourg, and France. To the east lie Poland and the Czech Republic. Germany has coasts that touch the Baltic Sea in the northeast and the North Sea in the northwest.

⊙ Topography

The major land regions of Germany run in roughly parallel, east-west bands across the country. Ancient glaciers (ice masses) once covered the largest and northernmost region, the North German Plain. As the

glaciers melted, they left behind flat lowlands, small lakes, and heaths (areas of sandy, infertile soil). Broad rivers flow northward through the plain, and swamps and bogs have formed in areas of poor drainage. Off the northwestern coast of Germany are the flat, sandy East Frisian and North Frisian Islands.

Although much of the soil in the North German Plain is too poor for crop production, livestock graze on pastures in the region, and local tree farms supply Germany's lumber mills. The southern edge of the plain contains fertile areas known as *borden*, where farmers can raise a variety of grain and vegetable crops.

More than a dozen small mountain ranges rise within the Central Highlands, a region stretching across the middle of Germany. Brocken, a mountain peak, reaches 3,747 feet (1,142 meters) within the Harz range, which straddles the old boundary between East and West Germany. Dense woodlands, including the Thuringian and Bohemian Forests, cover the mountains and the broad valleys to the south. The

The Bavarian Alps in southern Germany are part of the largest mountain range in Europe.

fertile Thuringian Basin, in eastern Germany, ends at the Ore Mountains on the border of the Czech Republic.

Long, wooded ridges are common in the South German Hills. The steep Swabian Jura (highland) runs north of the Danube River near the river's source in southwestern Germany. The Franconian Jura, the Steigerwald, and other highlands rise above plateaus and winding river valleys. The clay soil of the region provides fertile farmland. The mountainous Black Forest, in southwestern Germany, takes its name from the thick forests of fir and spruce trees that cover the hillsides.

The Alpine Forelands (foothills) begin south of the Danube and continue to the Bavarian Alps, which rise along Germany's borders with Switzerland and Austria. Ancient glaciers formed many lakes in southern Bavaria, an area of rapid streams, rolling foothills, pastures, and fields of wheat and other grains. Southwest of Munich—the largest city in southern Germany—rises Zugspitze, the country's highest point at 9,721 feet (2,963 m).

◎ Rivers and Lakes

For centuries Germany's waterways provided an important transportation link for its many principalities and trading centers. German cities used the rivers to ship their products to market, and the more powerful states collected river tolls, or payment for passage. In modern times, a system of canals has brought many of Germany's major rivers into a Europeanwide shipping network.

The Rhine River rises in the Swiss Alps, flows northward, and for many miles forms a natural border between Germany and its neighbors Switzerland and France. After passing through the industrial Ruhr region of western Germany, the river enters the Netherlands and empties into the North Sea, an arm of the Atlantic Ocean.

One of the busiest water routes in the world, the Rhine accommodates some 9,000 cargo vessels each month. Commercial boats can navigate about 500 miles (800 km) of the Rhine's 820-mile (1,320-km) length. Cruise ships and sightseeing boats carry vacationers up and down the river to view the castles, villages, and vineyards of the Rhine valley.

A canal links the Rhine to the Main and Danube Rivers, allowing ships to travel from the North Sea to the Black Sea in southeastern Europe. The Danube passes through southern Germany before crossing into Austria. Engineers have built canals and deep channels that enable barges to navigate the river's course.

The rivers of the North German Plain empty into either the North Sea or the Baltic Sea, which are linked by the Kiel Canal. The Weser River passes the busy port of Bremen, and the Elbe flows through Hamburg before widening into a broad estuary (an arm of

The fertile banks of the **Rhine River** in western Germany have supported agriculture for centuries.

the sea at the lower end of a river). Canals join the Rhine with these two waterways and with the Oder River, part of which divides Germany from Poland.

The glaciers that once covered Germany carved many basins in which small lakes formed. Lake Müritz, Lake Schwerin, and several other glacial lakes dot the North German Plain. Germany, Switzerland, and Austria line the shores of Lake Constance (also known as the Bodensee). The level of the lake rises in the spring, when ice and snow melt in the nearby Alps and flow into the lake.

THE BODENSEE

The Bodensee *(above)*, or Lake Constance, is one of Germany's largest freshwater lakes. It is 40 miles (64 km) long and 8.5 miles (14 km) wide, covering a total of 220 square miles (570 sq. km). More than 4.5 million Germans, Austrians, and Swiss rely on the lake for drinking water. Some 250,000 birds make their homes there, and 30 different species of fish live in the lake's waters.

Climate

Extreme temperatures are rare in Germany, which has a mild continental climate. Easterly winds bring warm summers and cool winters to the plains of eastern Germany. Temperatures in the capital of Berlin, a northeastern city, average 73°F (23°C) in July, the warmest month, and 34°F (1°C) in January, the coldest month. The weather is milder in western Germany, where winds blowing from the Atlantic Ocean heat the air in the winter and cool it in summer.

The unusual weather phenomenon known as the Föhn causes rapid weather changes in southern Germany. It occurs when warm tropical air flows across the Alps, losing moisture on the southern slopes of the mountains. As the air descends from the cold peaks, it quickly warms, evaporating cloud cover and melting snow. The rapid change in weather causes many southern Germans to experience headaches, irritability, and circulatory problems.

Highland regions, including the Harz Mountains and the Bavarian Alps, often experience below-freezing winter temperatures. The high altitude of the Alps shortens the mountain summers, but an Alpine wind called the Föhn can bring warm, clear weather to southern Germany in any season. Temperatures in Munich average 73°F (23°C) in July and 28°F (2°C) in January.

Rain falls throughout the year in the northwest, but farther inland most rain occurs in summer. The mountains of the south may receive more than 80 inches (203 centimeters) of rain and snow a year, while about 30 inches (76 cm) of precipitation fall annually in the Central Highlands. During winter, ice may clog some of Germany's seaports, and snow blankets the peaks and valleys of the Bavarian Alps.

Flora and Fauna

Centuries of settlement and farming have greatly reduced Germany's woodlands. Natural forests and cultivated plantations cover only about one-third of the land. Pine trees grow in the sandy soil of the coastal region, while stands of spruce dominate the woods of the Central Highlands. Silver firs flourish in the mountains of the south and in the Black Forest.

Strict laws require that all trees harvested for timber in Germany must be replaced. Nevertheless, the nation's forests diminished during the 1980s, when air pollution and acid rain caused many trees to lose their foliage and die. A 1999 study showed that 22 percent of the country's tree stocks had been damaged by air pollution. The German government has sought to alleviate this problem by implementing laws to reduce airborne pollutants.

Little ground vegetation surrounds Germany's tree plantations, but the country's natural forests contain heather, mosses, and lichens. Broom, juniper, and bracken plants grow in the heaths of the north. During late spring, wildflowers color the slopes of the Bavarian Alps.

Germany is home to many native species of animals and birds. Deer, lynx, pine martens, and grouse live in the country's forests. Beavers

The lynx, a powerful cat, is native to Germany and much of northern Europe.

inhabit the Elbe valley, and wild boars and deer roam the woodlands of Bavaria. The Lüneburg Heath and many of the surrounding heaths in the North German Plain are protected game reserves. A 5,680-acre (2,299-hectare) area along Lake Schaal in eastern Germany is inhabited by sea eagles, cranes, cormorants, ospreys, and other birds.

Natural Resources

Germany has a variety of natural resources, but coal is the only mineral found in large quantities. The Ruhr contains major deposits of coal, although mining operations have exhausted many of the largest pits in the region. Coal also exists in the Saar region west of the Rhine River. Workers mine lignite (brown) coal near Cologne in the Rhine valley, in Bavaria, and in eastern Germany. Yet the country has also sought to reduce its dependence on such "dirty" energy-producing fuels as coal, focusing on solar and wind power. Since the mid-1990s, Germany has been the world's leading producer of wind energy.

The Harz Mountains and the Thuringian Forest contain significant deposits of iron ore, an important ingredient of steel production. Deposits of potash east of the Harz region make Germany one of the world's largest suppliers of this valuable fertilizer. Engineers have discovered oil reserves near the North Sea coasts, but Germany still must import most of its oil and natural gas.

Germany's other natural resources include rock salt, copper, lead, silver, tin, uranium, zinc, and bauxite (the raw material of aluminum). Artisans use kaolin, a fine white clay, to make the country's famous Dresden china.

Berlin

Located on Germany's northeastern plains, Berlin (population 3.4 million) began in the 1200s as the two towns of Berlin and Kölln. Lying on opposite banks of the Spree River, these busy trade centers merged in

1397. In 1701 Berlin became the administrative hub of the German kingdom of Prussia. After the founding of the German Empire in 1871, the city served as the national capital until 1945.

After Germany's defeat in World War II, four foreign powers—the United States, Britain, France, and the Soviet Union—occupied Berlin. The city was later divided into eastern and western sectors. East Berlin became the capital of Communist East Germany. West Berlin remained part of West Germany, although it was cut off from the rest of that country.

The Communist government built a massive wall around West Berlin in 1961 to prevent East Germans from fleeing to West Germany. In 1989, when the East German government opened its borders, the Berlin Wall was destroyed. Soon the two Germanys reunited, and the nation transferred the federal government back to Berlin from Bonn, in western Germany.

Although World War II bombing heavily damaged the city, a few landmarks survived. The State Opera House and the State Library date to the 1700s. The imposing Reichstag was built in the late nineteenth century as the seat of Germany's parliament. Near the Kurfürstendamm, the main street of western Berlin, stand the walls of the Kaiser Wilhelm Church. Partially destroyed by bombing, the church's ruins were left in place as a powerful reminder of the war.

A major manufacturing center, Berlin produces electronics, machinery,

chemicals, steel, clothing, textiles, and rubber goods. A canal links a busy industrial port on the Spree River to the North and Baltic Seas. The capital also has important civilian and military airports and is a major railroad hub for northern Europe.

Secondary Cities

Germany's cities began growing rapidly in the 1800s, as new industries attracted job seekers from the countryside. Although many urban centers were heavily damaged during World War II, the postwar recovery, especially in West Germany, allowed the large cities to rebuild. City dwellers make up 87 percent of the total German population—one of the highest urban concentrations in Europe.

Hamburg (population 1.7 million) lies on the Elbe River in northwestern Germany. The city was founded as Hammaburg in A.D. 810 by the emperor Charlemagne. In the twelfth century, Hamburg joined the Hanseatic League, a trade association of northern European cities. Although the league later disbanded, Germany's principal seaport has kept its historic name as the Free and Hanseatic City of Hamburg.

Shipyards, ironworks, steelworks, sawmills, and manufacturing facilities operate in Hamburg's industrial areas. Other plants make chemicals and optical instruments. Although the city has large fac-

"ICH BIN EIN BERLINER"

In August 1963, U.S. president John F. Kennedy made a historic visit to West Berlin. Kennedy's visit and his subsequent speech were meant to encourage West Berliners, surrounded by the Berlin Wall and isolated from the Western world. Unwittingly, Kennedy's speech also amused the huge crowd that witnessed it. In a dramatic moment, Kennedy expressed his unity with West Berliners by exclaiming in German, "Ich bin ein Berliner!" which he thought meant, "I am a Berliner"—a citizen of Berlin. However, the president had misspoken. He should have said, "Ich bin Berliner." By adding the word *ein*, he had, in fact, called himself a very different kind of Berliner—a jelly doughnut.

The ruined tower of **Kaiser Wilhelm Church** *(center, rear)* contrasts with modern buildings in downtown Berlin. A new tower *(center, front)* was added to the church in the early 1960s.

tory districts and extensive port facilities, nearly half of its land is covered with greenery and parks.

The capital of Bavaria, Munich (population 1.2 million) is known as München to German speakers. The city enjoys a lively cultural life and supports concert halls, jazz clubs, art galleries, and theaters. It is also a center of Germany's huge beer industry. Oktoberfest, Munich's annual beer festival, attracts visitors from around the world. The city also produces automobiles, aircraft, and electronic equipment.

Cologne (population 963,000), one of Germany's oldest cities, was first settled by the Ubii, an ancient Germanic group. The most famous landmark of Cologne (known as Köln to German speakers) is a towering cathedral that took more than 600 years to complete. The city's factories make chemicals, textiles, automobiles, and chocolate. Eau de Cologne, a well-known fragrance, was invented in Cologne in the eighteenth century.

Many Habsburg emperors were crowned in the cathedral of Frankfurt am Main (population 643,000), but this city on the Main River also served as the seat of Germany's first elected parliament. An important commercial and industrial hub, Frankfurt has factories that make leather goods, chemicals, and pharmaceuticals. Germany's central bank and stock exchange have their headquarters in Frankfurt, which has become the nation's financial capital. The European Central Bank is also based there. An international book

Frankfurt am Main's towering skyscrapers have earned it the nickname "Mainhattan." The city is one of Europe's main industrial and business centers.

The Zwinger is Dresden's most famous building. It is a stunning example of the elaborate Baroque style of architecture.

fair in the city attracts thousands of editors, writers, and publishers each year.

Settled in the tenth century, Dresden (population 456,000) later served as the capital of Saxony, a powerful German state. A city of fine churches and imposing palaces, Dresden also became a manufacturing center in the late 1800s. But the city was devastated in February 1945, when air raids reduced most of Dresden's buildings to rubble. Architects are painstakingly rebuilding many churches and monuments. Since 1713, factories in the nearby town of Meissen (Meißen) have produced the world famous Dresden china, the first porcelain made in Europe. The city and its neighboring region were devastated by floods in the summer of 2002. The floods killed sixteen people and caused billions of dollars in damage.

About 60 miles (96 km) northwest of Dresden is Leipzig (population 442,000), which occupies a strategic junction of rivers and railroads. An early center of the German publishing industry, Leipzig also hosts trade fairs that attract manufacturers from throughout the world. Factories in the city produce steel, chemicals, plastics, and clothing.

 To find out more about Berlin and other cities in Germany, go to vgsbooks.com.

HISTORY AND GOVERNMENT

As early as one hundred thousand years ago, nomadic hunting groups migrated into the forests and river valleys of north central Europe. The remains of one of these early hunters have been found in the Neander Valley near Düsseldorf in western Germany. The discovery led scientists to name these prehistoric people Neanderthals.

By 400 B.C., groups of Celts had settled much of central Europe, including southern and western Germany. They raised grains and livestock and crafted iron tools and weapons for use in farming and in warfare.

○ Teutonic Settlers and Early Kingdoms

Around 100 B.C., northern European peoples known as Teutons migrated southward into Germany, pushing aside the Celts. At the same time, the armies of Rome, an expanding empire based on the Italian Peninsula, were conquering Celtic groups west of the Rhine

River. This mighty waterway later divided the Roman province of
Gaul (modern France) and Germania, the Roman name for Teutonic
lands lying east of the Rhine.

By the fourth century A.D., raids from Germania were weakening
Rome. In A.D. 395, the empire was divided into eastern and western
halves. Many of the Germanic groups—including the Goths and the
Franks—saw this as an opportunity to press their attacks. In 410 the
Goths invaded Italy, burning and pillaging the city of Rome, the
capital of the western empire.

To strengthen his forces, the Roman emperor Honorius hired
Germanic soldiers to serve in the Roman army under Germanic commanders. But Odoacer, one of these leaders, turned against Rome in
476. As his troops attacked the capital, Odoacer deposed the emperor
and became the ruler of Italy. The western empire collapsed, and
the Franks and other Germanic groups began crossing the Rhine and
seizing Roman territory in Gaul.

Charlemagne, or Charles the Great, is the most famous of all medieval European kings. A towering figure, he had a sharp mind and powerful personality.

In 486 the Frankish king Clovis defeated the Roman governor who was still ruling in Gaul. After his victory, Clovis established the Frankish Empire, a realm that stretched across much of northern Europe. He also converted his subjects to Christianity, a faith introduced to Europe from the Middle East. In religious matters, the Franks submitted to the Roman Catholic pope, the head of the Christian church in Rome.

Charlemagne, who became the ruler of the Franks in 768, greatly expanded his realm in central and western Europe. In 800 Pope Leo III crowned Charlemagne as "Emperor of the Romans," and the Frankish king became the ruler of a revived western empire. For a few years, Charlemagne united the Germanic peoples and ended the frequent warfare and invasions in western Europe.

During the ninth century, raiders from the east staged several attacks on German territory east of the Rhine. King Ludwig II called upon German nobles to defend the realm. For their help, the German nobles received titles and land. Gradually, these nobles, or dukes, created independent duchies within Germany. The largest and most powerful duchies were Saxony, Swabia, Franconia, Bavaria, and Lorraine.

The Holy Roman Empire

In 919, after the dynasty begun by Charlemagne had died out, the Frankish and Saxon nobles elected the Saxon duke Henry I as the king of Germany. Henry brought the five largest German duchies into a strong alliance. His son, Otto I, claimed extensive new lands to the west and south for the kingdom.

A brilliant military strategist, Otto stopped an invasion of his realm by the nomadic Magyars in 955. Heeding a call for help by the pope, whose lands were also threatened by invasion, Otto led his forces into Italy in 962. In gratitude, the pope crowned Otto as the first Holy Roman emperor. For centuries after this event, the kings of Germany also became the leaders of the Holy Roman Empire.

Under Otto's successors, the Holy Roman Empire included hundreds of large and small territories, each ruled by a member of the German nobility. The nobles—who had their own courts, laws, and armed forces—also had the power to elect the king.

In the mid-1100s, however, Germany was united briefly under Frederick I. Nicknamed Barbarossa (meaning "red-beard"), Frederick was a strong, daring leader who became king in 1152 and Holy Roman emperor three years later. Through military force and negotiation, Frederick extended his rule to parts of what have become Poland and Hungary. Frederick's ambitious son Henry VI also brought northern Italy into the realm.

Under Frederick I and his son, trade and industry increased along Germany's seacoast and in lands adjoining the Rhine River. As these trading centers grew and prospered, they became wealthy enough to break free of the German princes and to become independent cities.

In 1273 the German princes elected Rudolf I, a member of the powerful Habsburg family, as their king. Rudolf added to Habsburg lands by seizing Austria, a duchy lying southeast of Germany along the Danube River. Through conquests and marriage alliances, the Habsburgs greatly enlarged the territory under their control.

In the fourteenth century, Charles IV, the Habsburg king and Holy Roman emperor, issued a law called the Golden Bull. This law codified an old tradition in which seven German electors had the power to choose the Holy Roman emperor. The law

THE BLACK DEATH

In the mid-1300s, a devastating outbreak of bubonic plague swept across Europe. By the year 1400, the plague had killed some 40 million Europeans—perhaps half or more of the continent's population. The roots of the plague are not known for sure, but medical historians believe that the disease may have come on trading ships traveling from central Asia. Regardless of how the pandemic (widespread epidemic) started, it spread quickly. Carried by rats and fleas, it could be transmitted to a person by a flea bite. Once infected, the victim experienced painful swelling in the legs, neck, armpits, or groin. A high fever, rapid pulse, and body aches brought a painful end to the victim's life—often within five days of the first symptoms.

increased the power of the electors, whose lands could not be divided. The electors soon became the wealthiest rulers in the empire.

In 1438 the electors chose Albert II, a member of the Habsburg dynasty, as emperor. For the next five centuries, the imperial title would remain with the Habsburgs, who controlled Austria and other principalities that made up the realm's largest and strongest domain.

The Protestant Reformation

Important changes occurred in Germany in the fifteenth century, when a revival of ancient arts and philosophy called the Renaissance arrived from Italy. The first university within the lands of modern-day Germany had been founded in the previous century in Heidelberg, in 1386. In the following decades, universities were founded in Cologne, Leipzig, Freiburg, and other cities. The Renaissance scholars in the new German universities pressed for changes in the powerful Roman Catholic Church. These men deemed the Church and its leaders corrupt and out of touch with the general population. One of these reformers, a German priest named Martin Luther, attacked the practices of the Church, which banned him in 1521. Many people in northern Germany, however, were joining Luther's call for reform. His followers, who were known as Protestants, established the Lutheran

Martin Luther called for reform of the Catholic Church, leading to major religious, political, and cultural changes throughout Europe.

Church in the 1520s. Soon the Protestant Reformation was sweeping across northern Europe.

By 1555 a majority of Germans—including townspeople, nobles, and peasants—had become Protestants. Several northern German princes used the Reformation as an excuse to seize lands owned by the Catholic Church. Facing a dangerous rebellion, the Catholic Habsburg emperor Charles V signed the Peace of Augsburg. This pact gave the rulers of the empire's many realms the right to choose the religion to be practiced in their state.

During the next few decades, new Protestant sects were established in Germany, the Netherlands, and Switzerland. These Reformed churches rejected both Lutheran and Catholic practices. In addition, the Roman Catholic Church won back much of southern Germany, as well as Austria and Bohemia (a kingdom lying north of Austria). The Church had a strong ally in the Habsburg dynasty, whose members were loyal Catholics. But in 1618, an attempt by the Habsburgs to place a Catholic on the throne of Bohemia led to a violent uprising. This touched off a thirty-year conflict between Europe's Protestants and Catholics.

During the Thirty Years' War, German princes attacked their rivals, and foreign armies marched across central Europe to seize and plunder German lands. Allying with the Protestants, the king of Sweden led an invasion of Germany's Baltic coast. French leaders sent troops across the Rhine to fight against their rivals, the Habsburgs.

The war ended in 1648, when Protestant and Catholic leaders agreed to the Peace of Westphalia. The truce officially recognized Catholic and Protestant territories in Germany. Habsburg authority over the Protestant states ended, although members of the Habsburg dynasty still held the title of Holy Roman emperor.

The Rise of Prussia

The Peace of Westphalia strengthened the rulers of Saxony, Bavaria, Brandenburg, Prussia, and other large German states. Many of these princes began to play an important role in European conflicts over trade and territory. Meanwhile, the power of the Habsburg rulers—whose domain came to be known as Austria—began to decline.

By the early eighteenth century, the Hohenzollern dynasty was ruling the combined territories of Prussia and Brandenburg in northern Germany. In 1740 Frederick II (the Great), the king of Prussia, invaded and occupied Silesia, a mineral-rich region ruled by the Habsburgs.

Rivalry over Silesia sparked another conflict between Austria and Prussia in 1756. Frederick led his armies against Austria and its many allies, which included Russia, France, Bavaria, and Saxony. The high

Frederick II (the Great) of Prussia was a successful soldier and cunning diplomat.

cost of this Seven Years' War forced Maria Theresa, the Habsburg empress, to ask for peace terms in 1763. By the Treaty of Hubertusburg, Prussia kept Silesia. Later the Hohenzollerns expanded their realm across northern Germany, creating the largest and most powerful German state.

Napoleonic Wars and the German Confederation

In the early 1790s, a popular revolution in France brought down the country's king. Europe's rulers, who feared rebellion in their own lands, were soon at war with the French revolutionary armies. The French crossed the Rhine to occupy German principalities and to spread antimonarchical sentiment among the German people.

The French general Napoleon Bonaparte took command of his nation in 1799. Napoleon invaded Germany and defeated the Prussian and Austrian armies sent to fight him. In 1806 Napoleon organized his German conquests into the Confederation of the Rhine, an action that destroyed the Holy Roman Empire.

The armies of Prussia, Austria, and Russia defeated the French in 1813 at Leipzig. Prussia and Britain routed Napoleon two years later at the Battle of Waterloo and forced the French leader into exile.

The victorious nations then met at the Congress of Vienna to redraw the boundaries of Europe. The congress also reorganized the German kingdoms, duchies, and principalities into the thirty-four states and four cities of the new German Confederation.

Although the confederation established a national parliament, the Bundestag, this legislature had little authority. Each state within the German Confederation enforced its own laws, coined its own money, collected its own taxes, and raised its own armies. In 1834 a customs union was established among most of the German states.

Poor harvests during the 1840s led to food shortages and economic problems. Many Germans demanded the formation of a truly democratic government. In 1848 an uprising in France sparked riots in Austria and Germany. The rulers of Prussia, Bavaria, and other German states then agreed to establish a new assembly in Frankfurt.

The members of this legislature proposed a constitution in which Germany would be united under a hereditary emperor. The assembly offered the title of emperor to Frederick William, the king of Prussia. But Frederick William—who strongly opposed the assembly—refused the title. The assembly gradually lost support and was dissolved in 1849.

Unification

In 1862 Frederick William's successor, King Wilhelm I, appointed Otto von Bismarck as his prime minister. Bismarck sought the unification of Germany under Prussia's leadership.

LUDWIG II, KING OF BAVARIA

Ludwig II (1845–1886) stands as one of the most peculiar monarchs in German history. Born into the Wittelsbach family that had ruled Bavaria since the 1100s, he would become the family's last king. By the time he ascended to the throne in 1864, his office held little power. Government ministers and the Bavarian parliament dictated the kingdom's policies. This situation allowed Ludwig to pursue his own private interests, which included architecture and music. He spent his family's fortune building three magnificent palaces—Linderhof Palace, Herrenchiemsee Palace, and Neuschwanstein Castle. A devoted follower of opera, he supported German composer Richard Wagner and built a spectacular opera hall at Bayreuth for performances of his work. As he grew older, Ludwig became increasingly eccentric, completely withdrawing from public life. Alarmed by his reckless spending, Ludwig's family and Bavarian ministers had him deposed in 1886. Shortly thereafter, he died under mysterious circumstances.

To reach this goal, he added to Prussia's territory through wars with Denmark and Austria. His victories in these conflicts gave Bismarck the authority he needed to replace the German Confederation with a new state, the North German Confederation, which Prussia dominated.

Otto von Bismarck

At the same time, a member of Prussia's Hohenzollern dynasty was offered the throne of Spain. France strongly objected to this proposal, fearing Hohenzollern domination of Europe as well as Prussia's growing military might. Seeing another opportunity to strengthen Prussia's status, Bismarck sparked the Franco-Prussian War in 1870. The war ended with the fall of Paris, the French capital, in 1871. After France surrendered, Bismarck forced the French government to make heavy war reparations (payments).

During the Franco-Prussian War, Bismarck brought the southern German states under Prussian control. Wilhelm assumed the leadership of a unified German Empire as Kaiser (emperor) Wilhelm I.

In the late nineteenth century, Germany experienced rapid growth. The population increased, and busy mines and factories transformed the nation's economy into an industrial powerhouse. Germany established colonies in Africa and Asia to match the growing international and colonial power of Britain and France.

Bismarck kept firm control over the legislature and tried to stamp out opposition to the Prussian monarchy. He also limited the activities of the Socialist Party, which championed the rights of Germany's industrial workers. But the rapid industrialization of the country fostered a strong labor movement and widespread support of Socialist politicians.

War and Defeat

Industrialization in Europe brought about an intense rivalry for land and trade among the European powers. Wilhelm II, who became Germany's ruler in 1888, ordered the construction of a powerful, modern navy. Germany, Austria, and Italy had already formed the Triple Alliance and had agreed to cooperate in case of war. Fearing Germany's military power, Russia, France, and Britain later signed the Triple Entente. The two competing blocs built up their forces and prepared for a continent-wide conflict.

In June 1914, the heir to the throne of Austria was murdered in Serbia, a region in southeastern Europe. Austria reacted by declaring war on Serbia, an ally of Russia. Because of their alliance, the nations of the Triple Entente quickly mobilized their forces. Germany also put its troops on a war footing to honor its alliance with Austria. In August Wilhelm II ordered an attack on France, an action that brought the two European alliances into the war that would come to be known as World War I.

Germany defeated Russia on the eastern front, while British, French, and, later, U.S. forces fought Germany to a stalemate in northern France. (The United States joined the war in 1917.) But eventually Wilhelm's commanders lost ground. In November 1918, Germany surrendered.

Kaiser Wilhelm gave up his throne, and the Socialists proclaimed the founding of a new, democratic German government. Under the postwar Treaty of Versailles, Germany surrendered much of eastern Prussia to Poland. The victorious Allies demanded huge reparations and occupied cities and industries in southeastern Germany.

The Weimar Republic and the Nazi Regime

In 1919 an assembly met in Weimar, a city in central Germany, to draw up a new constitution. Led by the Socialists, the assembly established a two-house parliament, an elected presidency, and the office of

German soldiers guard a trench during World War I. Some 1.75 million German servicemen died as a result of the war.

chancellor, whom the president would appoint. The assembly also ratified (accepted) the Treaty of Versailles.

Burdened by the heavy war reparations, the German economy collapsed during the 1920s. Unemployment rose, and raging inflation destroyed the value of German currency. As Germans lost faith in the country's leaders, small but violent political parties sprang up to fuel the turmoil. In 1923 the National Socialist (Nazi) Party, led by Adolf Hitler, attempted to stage a Putsch (overthrow) in Munich. Although the revolt failed and Hitler went to jail, he and the Nazi Party steadily gained support.

Under the leadership of President Paul von Hindenburg, the German economy improved in the late 1920s. But a worldwide economic depression that began in 1929 dealt another blow to the Weimar Republic. Street fighting among Nazis, Communists, and other groups increased.

Runaway inflation left the German economy in chaos in the 1920s. The government printed so much money that it became virtually worthless. In 1914 one U.S. dollar equaled the value of 4 German marks. By mid-1920, one dollar was the equal of 40 marks. A year-and-a-half later, one dollar was worth 200 marks. In early 1923, 18,000 marks equaled one dollar, and by the end of the year, inflation had exploded to the rate of 4.2 trillion marks to one single dollar.

After serving his short jail term, Hitler began giving public speeches in which he blamed Communists, Jews, and other groups for Germany's wartime defeat and for its economic problems. Many Germans agreed with these views, and the Nazi Party's power and popularity increased. Bowing to political pressure, Hindenburg appointed Hitler chancellor in 1933.

After Hindenburg's death in 1934, Hitler named himself Germany's Führer (leader) and took complete control of German industry, administration, and education. Jews and others whom the Nazis considered enemies of the regime lost their homes, businesses, jobs, and citizenship.

Germany rapidly strengthened its army and navy, denounced the Treaty of Versailles, and began claiming territory in neighboring nations. In 1939 Germany signed a pact with the Soviet Union, a vast Communist confederation to the east that was dominated by Russia. Although they agreed not to attack one another, these two countries secretly planned to invade and divide Poland. Fearing an attack, Poland mobilized its armies. When Hitler invaded Poland on

German Nazi troops march through Austria. Germany annexed its neighbor to the south in March 1938.

September 1, Britain and France declared war on Germany. Poland's poorly equipped forces were quickly defeated, and Germany and the Soviet Union occupied the country. World War II had begun.

World War II and Its Aftermath

After defeating Poland, Hitler ordered invasions of Denmark, Norway, Belgium, the Netherlands, and France. The German and Italian armies also overran southeastern Europe and much of North Africa. Hitler also broke the 1939 pact with the Soviet Union by invading Russia in 1941. In December 1941, Japan attacked the United States, which joined the Allies of France, Britain, and the Soviet Union in their war against the Axis (Germany and its allies).

By the winter of 1942, Germany had conquered most of Europe, including the western plains of the Soviet Union. In many occupied areas, the Germans seized industries, crop harvests, and natural resources and made conquered peoples work as slave laborers. As the war progressed, German forces herded Jews, Slavs, Roma (Gypsies), political and military prisoners, and others into concentration camps. Millions of inmates were put to death in what became known as the Holocaust.

But German armies were fighting on several fronts, and the United States was scoring victories against Japan in the Pacific theater of war. While Allied bombers destroyed German factories, railroads, and cities, counterattacks forced Germany out of the Soviet Union and North Africa. In June 1944, Allied armies invaded France and soon drove the Germans from Paris. With Soviet armies marching on Berlin and the war nearly lost, Hitler committed suicide on April 30, 1945. One week later, Germany formally surrendered.

Britain, France, the United States, and the Soviet Union divided the nation and capital of Berlin into occupation zones. With its industries destroyed and many of its cities in ruins, Germany had to depend on aid from its former enemies to survive and rebuild.

Visit vgsbooks.com for links to websites where you can learn more about the history of Germany, including its involvement in World War I, World War II, and the Holocaust.

Postwar Divisions

In 1948 the United States, France, and Britain merged their three occupation zones in western Germany while maintaining control over West Berlin. The Soviet Union still occupied eastern Germany and East Berlin. With Soviet forces backing them, German Communist and Socialist leaders formed the Socialist Unity Party and set up a government to administer the eastern zone.

The Allies allowed German politicians to establish a new, democratic government in Bonn. This city on the Rhine River became the capital of the Federal Republic of Germany (FRG, or West Germany) in 1949. The eastern sector of Berlin became the capital of the Soviet-controlled zone, where the German Communists founded the German Democratic Republic (GDR, or East Germany). Berlin remained divided into western and eastern halves. The West German government drew up a new constitution, and a parliament began meeting in Bonn. The legislature elected Konrad Adenauer, the leader of the Christian

Relentless **Allied bombing raids left much of Berlin in ruins by 1945.** More than one-third of the city was destroyed during World War II.

A German laborer helps rebuild West Berlin. Construction projects like this one were funded by **the Marshall Plan,** which enabled West Germany to make a full economic recovery by the early 1950s.

Democratic Union (CDU), as the Federal Republic's first chancellor.

Adenauer forged close economic and political ties with the nations of Western Europe. In 1955 West Germany joined the United States and several Western European nations in the North Atlantic Treaty Organization (NATO), a military alliance. Meanwhile, to help the war-ravaged nations of Europe and the new West German state, the United States adopted the Marshall Plan, a program of financial aid and investment.

In East Germany, the Communist government took control of banks, industries, farms, and private businesses. Walter Ulbricht, the general secretary (leader) of the Socialist Unity Party, remained East Germany's most powerful politician throughout the 1950s and 1960s. Under Ulbricht's guidance, East Germany became a founding member of the Warsaw Pact. This alliance of Europe's Communist nations also included the Soviet Union, Hungary, Poland, Czechoslovakia, Bulgaria, and Romania.

The Cold War

In 1955 the Allied occupation of Germany ended. Germany and Berlin became the dividing line in Europe between democratic countries allied with NATO and Communist nations allied with the Warsaw Pact. To prepare for any future conflict, the United States and the Soviet Union based large military forces and modern weaponry within Germany. This Cold War (nonviolent conflict) pitted the two blocs against one another and ended most trade and cooperation between them.

East Germany's economic recovery was slow compared to that of West Germany. The Communist government set wages and prices, so farmers and industrial workers had little incentive to increase their production to earn more money. Throughout the 1950s, as living standards remained low, millions of East Germans fled to the western sector of Berlin. In 1961, to prevent a further loss of its labor force, the Communist government closed its border with West Germany and built a heavily guarded concrete wall around West Berlin.

With the help of the Marshall Plan, the Federal Republic eventually became one of the richest and most productive nations in the world. Rebuilt factories produced industrial and consumer goods that found a global market. As living standards rose, millions of refugees and Gastarbeiter (guest workers) from southern Europe and Turkey arrived to meet the increased demand for factory labor.

THE STASI

The East German government kept a tight hold on its power by keeping a close watch on its citizens. Its State Security Service (the Staatssicherheitsdienst, usually referred to as the Stasi) employed more than 100,000 people full-time. Most of these persons were agents whose main job was to spy on East German citizens and record their activities. In addition, some 2 million East German civilians contributed information about their co-workers, neighbors, friends, and even family members to the Stasi. By closely monitoring the activities of its citizens, the East German government could easily quash any attempts to undermine its authority. And the fear of punishment by the government kept most East Germans from criticizing the regime.

Willy Brandt, a member of the Social Democratic Party, became West Germany's chancellor in 1969. Brandt's Ostpolitik (eastern policy) boosted trade and encouraged better relations with the nations of Eastern Europe. West Germany established diplomatic links with East Germany in 1973. In the same year, the two countries were admitted separately to the United Nations (UN).

In 1982 Helmut Kohl became West Germany's chancellor. Kohl maintained West Germany's ties to the East. In 1987 East German leader Erich Honecker paid a visit to his birthplace in West Germany. The visit symbolized the hope of many Germans for the reunification of their nation.

At the same time, many Communist nations of Eastern Europe were suffering economic decline and social unrest. Shortages of food, housing, and consumer goods angered industrial workers, while students and writers demanded more open governments. As the Soviet Union experienced its own political turmoil, its hold over the Warsaw Pact nations weakened.

These events undermined the

power of Eastern Europe's Communist leaders, including Erich Honecker. The growing unrest in East Germany forced Honecker to resign in October 1989. When Hungary allowed emigrants to cross freely into non-Communist Austria, thousands of East Germans began using this route to flee to West Germany. Unable to stop the migration, the East German government finally opened its borders to West Germany in November. Almost immediately, citizens of both East and West Germany began to tear down the Berlin Wall, which had become a symbol of divided Europe. As the Berlin Wall fell, millions of East Germans crossed into West Berlin.

Reunification

In March 1990, the East German Communists held open elections, which brought non-Communist political parties to power. Most East Germans favored adopting the economic and political system of West Germany, while most West Germans supported the reunification of the country. After a series of negotiations between leaders of the two states, Germany was formally reunified on October 3, 1990.

Reunification brought a nationwide celebration, as well as immediate economic problems. After losing government support, many inefficient East German businesses failed. Unemployment rose, and a housing shortage worsened. A flood of refugees in need of jobs and shelter arrived from southeastern Europe, where the fall of

Crowds gather to watch the historic dismantling of the Berlin Wall in November 1989. The East German border police had opened the wall's gates, creating a joyful mingling between East and West Germans.

To show their frustration with Germany's rising unemployment rate, protesters formed a human chain at this 1997 demonstration.

Communism had sparked unrest and civil war. Rising unemployment caused tension between immigrants and some ethnic Germans.

In November 1993, Germany became one of the twelve founding members of the European Union (EU), an organization of Western European nations that facilitates cooperation among its members in matters of trade, politics, and economics. (The European Union is the most recent incarnation of the European organization that began as the European Economic Community in 1957.)

In 1998 a new coalition of political parties, led by Gerhard Schröder, was elected to lead Germany. The new chancellor inherited a number of problems, including high unemployment rates and a struggling economy. The five former East German states continued to lag behind their neighbors, despite the transfer of hundreds of billions of dollars in cash from the western states since unification. In 1999 the euro, the new EU currency, began replacing the German deutsche mark. (The replacement process was completed at the beginning of 2002.)

Recent Events

After a brief boom in the late 1990s and 2000, the German economy staggered again in 2001. Sluggish growth has been due partly to an economic slowdown in the United States, one of Germany's largest trading partners. The global economic downturn that resulted from the September 11, 2001, terrorist attacks on the United States added to Germany's difficulties. Germany has also been a cooperating partner in the U.S. effort to track down the terrorists behind the infamous attacks.

In the September 2002 national elections, Schröder's party once again received a majority of seats. But the victory was narrow. It remains to be seen whether or not Germany's different political parties will work together to find solutions to the country's economic stagnation or whether the lack of strong support for a single political party or philosophy will result in gridlock and more economic difficulties in the future. Generous social welfare packages and extensive worker benefits have given Germans one of the world's highest standards of living. But these same benefits have also meant high taxes that slow economic growth. Serious economic reforms

Gerhard Schröder

are needed, but it is uncertain whether Germany's citizens and their political leaders are willing to make the sacrifices necessary for Germany to remain one of the world's most prosperous nations.

Government

The 1949 constitution of the Federal Republic (West Germany) governs the unified nation of Germany. Representatives of the German Länder (states) and members of the Bundestag, or parliament, meet every five years to elect the German president, the official head of state. A chancellor, who serves as the head of the German government, selects cabinet ministers and sets policy for nationwide concerns such as defense, foreign affairs, and the federal budget.

Citizens 18 years of age and older elect the 662 members of the Bundestag. The political party that holds a majority in the parliament may nominate the chancellor, who must win election by the entire chamber. The parliament debates important legislation and passes federal laws.

Representatives of the 16 German Länder sit on the Bundesrat, or federal council. The council allows the states to approve or reject laws that affect local governments. The heads of the state governments rotate as Bundesrat president, each serving a one-year term.

The German Länder have their own legislatures and constitutions. Although the states have the power to pass and enforce local laws, they also must observe statutes passed by the federal government. Länder governments administer health care, education, and environmental policies within their borders. Each state also has its own police force.

The Federal Constitutional Court is Germany's highest court. The Bundestag and Bundesrat each appoint eight judges to the court for 12-year terms. The court reviews laws and policies to make sure they conform to the country's constitution. Five federal courts have the power to review decisions by the local courts. Länder courts hear civil and criminal cases, and lower courts decide administrative disputes.

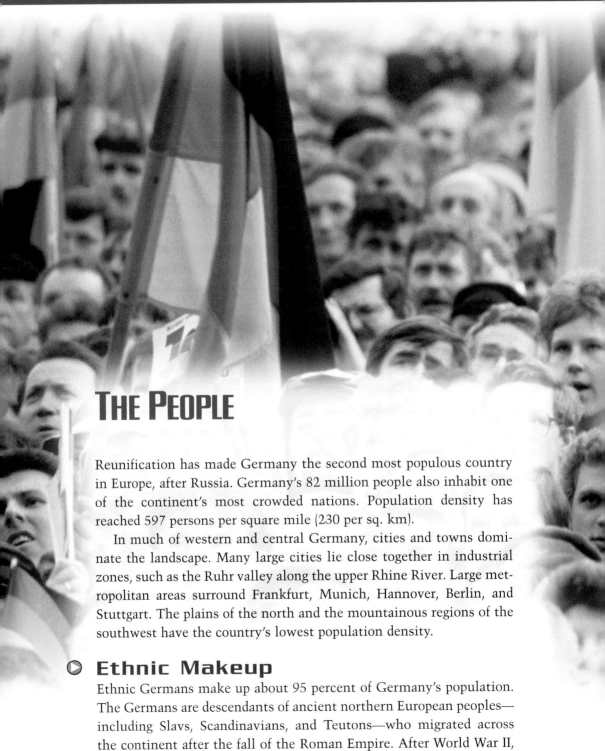

THE PEOPLE

Reunification has made Germany the second most populous country in Europe, after Russia. Germany's 82 million people also inhabit one of the continent's most crowded nations. Population density has reached 597 persons per square mile (230 per sq. km).

In much of western and central Germany, cities and towns dominate the landscape. Many large cities lie close together in industrial zones, such as the Ruhr valley along the upper Rhine River. Large metropolitan areas surround Frankfurt, Munich, Hannover, Berlin, and Stuttgart. The plains of the north and the mountainous regions of the southwest have the country's lowest population density.

Ethnic Makeup

Ethnic Germans make up about 95 percent of Germany's population. The Germans are descendants of ancient northern European peoples— including Slavs, Scandinavians, and Teutons—who migrated across the continent after the fall of the Roman Empire. After World War II,

Germany also welcomed people from southern Europe, Turkey, the Middle East, and Africa. Many of these immigrants arrived to fill new factory jobs created by Germany's expanding economy.

In the early 1990s, additional immigrants arrived as Communist regimes fell and as strict border controls ended in Eastern Europe. A civil war among Croats, Serbs, and Bosnians in southeastern Europe also brought a wave of refugees to Germany. Immigrants number more than 10 million—about 8 percent of the country's population. A majority of Germans feel that too many immigrants are moving to Germany. They are concerned that these newcomers are pushing down wages and placing a strain on the country's generous social welfare system.

Yet despite this influx, the population of Germany is declining. The current birthrate is 1.3 children per woman of childbearing age, and studies indicate that Germany's population may drop to some 66 million by the 2050s. This situation alarms German citizens and their political leaders. The decline of the native German population has raised fears that the traditional German culture and way of life may be on the wane. In coming decades, Germany's declining population will need a young labor force to keep its economy strong and to pay for the country's expensive social welfare programs. Immigration will likely be a key political issue in Germany in the years ahead.

Language

German is a member of the Germanic family of languages, which also includes Norwegian, Swedish, Dutch, Danish, and English. Modern German is spoken throughout Germany and Austria and in parts of Switzerland and France. Ethnic Germans living in Romania, Hungary, Poland, and the republics of the former Soviet Union also use German dialects.

By translating the Bible from Hebrew and Greek into German, Martin Luther created a standard written and spoken dialect known as Hochdeutsch, or High German. All of the country's broadcast and print media use a form of High German. Plattdeutsch, or Low German, is commonly heard in northern Germany. Other dialects survive in more isolated rural areas, such as Swabia in southwestern Germany. Residents of the Frisian Islands speak a unique blend of Dutch and German. Yiddish (a High German language written in Hebrew characters), which originated in Germany, has survived among Jews living in Europe, North America, and the Middle East. In eastern Germany, some ethnic Slavs use German and Slavic words.

UMLAUTS

The two dots over a vowel in certain German words are called umlauts. They represent a certain pronunciation of that vowel. For example, the u in the German word *Hummel* (bumblebee) has the same sound as the *u* in the English word *put*. The *ü* in the German word *Hüte* (hat), however, sounds like the *u* in the English word *unity*, except without the *y* sound at the beginning. Some publications do not include umlauts when printing German words in English. In most such cases, an *e* is added after the vowel that would normally receive an umlaut. For example, German chancellor Gerhard Schröder's name is often spelled Schroeder in English-language publications. If you'd like to learn some basic German words and phrases, go to vgsbooks.com for links to websites about the German language.

Health

Germans enjoy good health and an extensive health-care system. Nearly 11 percent of Germany's gross domestic product (GDP), the amount of goods produced within a

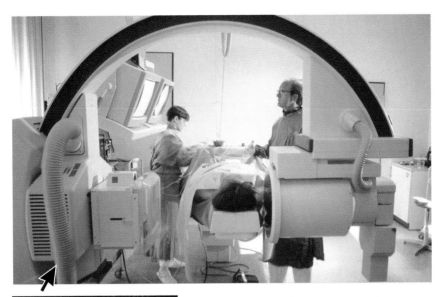

A patient at a Hamburg clinic gets a brain scan. Ninety percent of Germans belong to the state's health insurance system.

country in a year, is spent on health care. This percentage is second only to the United States's 14 percent. Life expectancy in Germany is 78 years, which is average for western European countries. Infant mortality—the number of babies who die before their first birthday—stands at 4.4 deaths for every 1,000 births, slightly below the western European average of 5 deaths. A federal system provides health insurance for workers, unemployed people, and retirees. Germans suffering from chronic diseases or who are disabled receive financial assistance.

Heart disease and cancer are the primary causes of death among Germans. A recent study by a German health advisory council criticized the traditional German diet, which is rich in fats and carbohydrates and lacks fruits and vegetables. Per capita consumption of fruits

The traditional German diet includes foods high in fat, such as **sausages.**

and vegetables in Germany is among the lowest of all western European countries. But many Germans, especially younger ones, are making healthy eating a priority. Cigarette smoking is prevalent in German society—a 1999 study found that nearly 25 percent of Germans are daily smokers. This percentage is about average in comparison to western European countries. To combat the problem, the European Commission kicked off a multimillion-dollar antismoking campaign in May 2002. The campaign targets young people between the ages of twelve to eighteen and seeks to discourage them from taking up smoking.

The human immunodeficiency virus (HIV) is also a concern, particularly in urban areas. The United Nations and the World Health Organization estimate that some 41,000 Germans are living with the virus that causes acquired immunodeficiency syndrome (AIDS).

Although Germany has about 295,000 doctors, rural areas suffer a shortage of physicians. Länder, local communities, and churches run most of Germany's 2,300 hospitals.

Education

Education in Germany begins in kindergarten, a voluntary preschool that accepts students between the ages of three and six. Children then enter a primary school known as a Grundschule, which lasts for four

German students receive a **broad and intensive education.** Germany's school systems are controlled by the individual Länder.

years. A German child's school day is relatively short, usually starting at 8 a.m. and ending at 1:30 or 2 p.m.

After the Grundschule, students have several options. They can attend a Gymnasium, a nine-year school that prepares them for university studies, or a Hauptschule, where they learn academic subjects and trades. Another option is the Realschule, which offers a slightly more advanced education than the Hauptschule. Graduates from a Hauptschule or Realschule often attend a vocational school that prepares them for careers in industry or business.

Before being admitted to a university, German students must first pass the Abitur, a difficult examination. About 28 percent of students go on to higher education, with nearly 16 percent graduating. Some 1.2 million students attend Germany's 91 universities, including the country's oldest, the University of Heidelberg, which was founded in 1386. All universities are state-run institutions that charge only a nominal tuition fee. Germany also has technical colleges, art institutes, music conservatories, theology schools, and continuing-education centers.

Women

For centuries, the role of women in Germany consisted primarily of bearing and raising children. Women had few rights under German law. They could not vote, sign legal documents, or work in a profession without their husbands' permission. They had few educational opportunities. Women who were forced to work out of necessity (usually for wages far lower than their male counterparts) were considered socially inferior.

A women's emancipation movement began to take root in Germany in the mid-1800s, as more and more German women sought alternatives to traditional roles. This movement focused on gaining rights for women,

WOMEN OF THE RUBBLE

When Germany surrendered to Allied forces in May 1945, the country lay in ruins. As so many men had been killed and wounded in the fighting, much of the task of cleaning up and rebuilding the country was undertaken by German women. These women, who became known as the Trümmerfrauen, or "women of the rubble," tended to the wounded, cleaned streets and bombed out buildings, and sorted bricks to repair homes. In the years following the war, the term Trümmerfrauen referred to the entire generation of women who did important but traditionally masculine jobs, such as working in mines, factories, and building construction. These women saved Germany from complete collapse and helped to rebuild the nation and return it to prosperity.

This poster proclaiming **"women's right to vote"** was created by the Social Democratic Party of Germany. It shows a woman waving a red banner in celebration of Women's Day on March 8, 1914.

including improving educational opportunities and securing the right to vote. German women were pressed into the workforce during World War I and were given the right to vote in 1918. But these changes did not lead to more women's rights. In the 1930s, Hitler's Nazi regime encouraged women to once again embrace their traditional roles.

Following World War II, the roles of women in the divided Germany took different directions. In the East, Soviet Communism required women to be an integral part of the workforce. This ideology, combined with mass defections of workers to West Germany, led to 90 percent of East German women working outside of the home. Educational and vocational opportunities were made available as never before.

In West Germany, equal rights for women came more slowly. Postwar prosperity meant that the majority of families did not need two incomes. The traditional women's role continued to be encouraged. Educational and career opportunities were more limited for women in West Germany. But in the 1970s, women's emancipation movements began to gather momentum. In 1977 women were granted equal rights in marriage. This gave them the right to file for divorce and to work outside the home without their husbands' permission. (Before these rights were in place, West German women could be dismissed from their jobs if their husbands demanded it.)

Reunification has had a particularly deep impact on women in the former East Germany. High unemployment in the new states has left many women jobless. Eastern Germans have also struggled with the loss of the comprehensive day care system they enjoyed under the Communist regime. Since most West German women did not work in the decades following World War II, the country has not developed a day care system that meets its current needs. To correct this problem, in 2002, Chancellor Gerhard Schröder proposed spending $4 billion over four years to increase day care availability.

In the 2000s, German women still struggle for equality in the workplace. A recent study showed that only 27 percent of German women hold managerial positions, tying Switzerland for the lowest percentage among European countries. In addition, many German women complain that society frowns on full-time working mothers. Many feel they have to make a choice between pursuing a career or raising a family.

CULTURAL LIFE

Germans are proud of their rich cultural heritage, a tradition that has given birth to some of the world's greatest writers, musicians, and artists. But they also carefully avoid nationalist sentiment, given the terrible crimes committed by Germans under the Nazi regime. Although a stronger national identity has emerged after reunification, many Germans still identify themselves by their home Länder—Bavarian or Saxon, for example—or as Europeans, more than as Germans.

▶ Religion

Religion has had a strong influence on Germany's art, politics, music, and literature. For centuries after the crowning of Otto I as the first Holy Roman emperor, Germany was closely tied to the Roman Catholic Church. Germany was also the birthplace of the Protestant Reformation, in which Martin Luther founded a new branch of Christianity and won a majority of Germans to Protestant churches.

By law people living in Germany may choose and practice any religion. The state provides financial support to the churches, which in turn offer a variety of social services, including preschool education and health care, to their members. Members also support their churches financially with a church tax of 8 to 9 percent of their income.

About 33 percent of Germans are members of Protestant sects, including Lutheran and Reformed traditions. Protestantism is strongest in the northern states of Germany. Roman Catholics, who form a majority in southern Germany, make up 33 percent of the total population. German society has become increasingly secular. Approximately 27 percent of Germans have either no religious affiliation or belong to unrecorded religious organizations. In the eastern states, where the Communist regime discouraged the practice of religion, less than 10 percent of the population belongs to a religious organization. Recent decades have seen more and more Germans abandoning their respective churches. Estimates show that only about

4 percent of German Protestants attend church services regularly, while only 17 percent of Catholics attend Mass on a weekly basis.

Germany's Jewish population numbered about 530,000 before the 1930s. After Hitler rose to power, however, the Nazi government closed synagogues (Jewish houses of prayer) and forced Jews out of their jobs and homes. Many Jews fled the country, and most who remained during World War II were arrested and executed. By the end of the war, only 30,000 Jews survived within Germany. In the 1990s, following the collapse of the Soviet Union, many Jews from the former Soviet republics emigrated to Germany. As a result, the Jewish population has grown rapidly in recent years. Approximately 82,000 Jews live in Germany.

About 3.2 million Muslims practice the Islamic faith in Germany. Most are ethnic Turks and North Africans who arrived in the country as guest workers. In recent years, many Muslim refugees have arrived from the former Yugoslavia.

Literature, Film, and Television

Scholars claim that the ninth-century *Hildebrandslied*, the story of a legendary hero, is the oldest literary work in the German language. Other myths and heroic tales of the early Germanic peoples were collected in the *Nibelungenlied*. Around A.D. 1200, many German knights penned epic poems about love and chivalry. Minnesingers—skilled composers and performers—wrote lyric poetry for performance at royal courts.

German writers flourished after the Protestant Reformation, when poetry, plays, and satirical novels became popular literary forms. Many of these authors used Italian or French works as their models. In the eighteenth century, Gotthold Ephraim Lessing and other writers described the events of their time in

Gotthold Ephraim Lessing revolutionized German drama. He also wrote many essays on literature and culture.

their works. Lessing's poetic drama *Nathan der Weise* included a strong appeal for religious tolerance. Young writers, including Johann Wolfgang von Goethe and Friedrich von Schiller, helped to create a national German literature.

Romantic writers of the 1800s based many of their works on fantasies and folklore. The brothers Jakob and Wilhelm Grimm brought out an edition of traditional children's fairy tales. Many German painters and musicians created works based on E. T. A. Hoffmann's stories of the supernatural. The writer Novalis—whose real name was Friederich von Hardenberg—authored essays and poetry filled with mystery and religious feeling.

Many German poets and philosophers of the nineteenth century took an interest in Europe's turbulent politics. Heinrich Heine wrote in support of the struggle against Europe's monarchies. Karl Marx and Friedrich Engels set forth the principles of Communism in *The Communist Manifesto*. Friedrich Nietzsche combined poetry and philosophy in his works, which criticized religious faith as well as modern German society.

Europe in the uncertain years before World War I provided the setting for Thomas Mann's *The Magic Mountain*. Hermann Hesse, who fled Germany in 1914 to become a Swiss citizen, incorporated Buddhism and other Asian ideas into *Steppenwolf* and other novels.

Determined to stamp out opposition to their regime, the Nazis banned the books of many prominent German writers. After World War II, Heinrich Böll and Günter Grass faced the legacy of Nazism in their stories and novels. The playwright Bertolt Brecht, who founded his own theater in Berlin, produced satirical plays with political subjects.

GOETHE'S CONTROVERSIAL BEST-SELLER

Legendary German writer Johann Wolfgang von Goethe's novel *Die Leiden des jungen Werthers (The Sorrows of Young Werther)* brought him international fame. The 1774 novel follows the exploits of a young man named Werther who falls in love with a woman who is engaged to be married to another man. When the passionate and immature Werther fails to win the woman's heart, he commits suicide. The story was based on a disappointing romance Goethe had experienced in his own life. However, some readers took the book too seriously. In seeking to emulate Werther, some young men committed suicide themselves, often quoting passages from the novel in their suicide notes. Goethe was deeply disturbed by this trend, and he spoke out against such acts.

Christa Wolf is another of Germany's most widely read authors. Her works, including *Was Bleibt (What Remains)*, describe contemporary life in eastern Germany.

On November 1, 1895, the world's first projected movie was shown in Berlin. Germany's capital was a hub for European filmmaking during the early decades of the industry. Directors such as Ernst Lubitsch, Fritz Lang, and F. W. Murnau (who directed *Nosferatu*, the first Dracula movie) made dark, psychological dramas that have strongly influenced later filmmakers. Actress and singer Marlene Dietrich enjoyed great popularity in her native Germany before emigrating to Hollywood, where she became an international star. In the 1930s, the Nazi regime took control of the German film industry. German films became an outlet for Nazi propaganda, and many of the industry's brightest minds left the country.

Marlene Dietrich

Many of the films created immediately after the war were known as Trümmerfilme (rubble films). These films dealt with Nazism and the war. In recent decades, a new generation of directors, known as the Young German Film movement, has brought new creative energy to the cinema. Volker Schlöndorff, Rainer Werner Fassbinder, and Wim Wenders have all created films that have won world acclaim.

German television viewers have a choice of two national public channels and a variety of stations run by the individual Länder. In addition, a wide variety of stations is available to viewers who subscribe to cable. These channels offer soap operas, situation comedies (including American shows dubbed in German), game shows, talk shows, sports, and music channels, including MTV. Germans living near the borders of other countries often receive broadcasts from their neighboring countries, and the large number of Turkish-speaking Germans also have access to Turkish-language channels.

Visit vgsbooks.com, where you can find links that have information about German culture and lifestyles.

Architecture, Art, and Music

Early German artists and architects borrowed freely from styles popular in other parts of Europe. Thirteenth-century architects adopted the

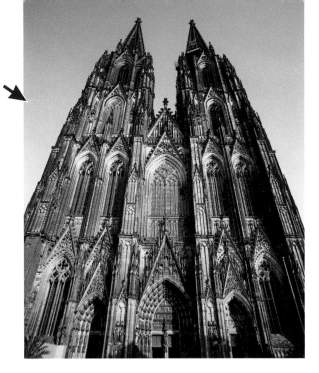

The Cologne Cathedral is a stunning example of Gothic architecture.

Gothic style of northern France to design cathedrals in Cologne and other German cities. Gothic builders used narrow stone buttresses (supports) to strengthen arched ceilings, high stone towers, and windows of stained glass. Painters of the Gothic period combined realistic details of everyday life with subjects from myths and fairy tales.

The Renaissance influenced many of Germany's sixteenth-century artists, including Albrecht Dürer. A master engraver, Dürer also produced portraits and still lifes on canvas. Dürer's works greatly inspired Lucas Cranach, who painted biblical scenes and created portraits of Martin Luther and other Protestant leaders. Matthias Grünewald decorated many German churches and cathedrals with his stained glass, paintings, and altarpieces.

German architects of the eighteenth century favored the elaborate Baroque style popular in France and Italy. Baroque churches and palaces exhibited ornate décor in gold leaf and brightly colored marble. Baroque painters enjoyed using mythological subjects in their large and detailed canvases.

German painters of the 1800s, including Caspar David Friedrich, turned to Romanticism, a style in which dark colors and serious subjects revealed the heroic inner struggles of the individual. In the early twentieth century, many German artists abandoned Romanticism for Expressionism. The painters Franz Marc, Otto Dix, and Max Beckmann expressed their emotions on canvas by using bright colors and strange, distorted shapes.

The need for extensive postwar rebuilding gave architects a chance to reshape German cities after World War II. One of the most important influences on modern designers was the Bauhaus, a school

The **Bauhaus style of architecture** rejected ornamentation, preferring pure geometrical designs. "Bauhaus" is a German term meaning "house for building."

founded in 1919 by the architect Walter Gropius. Bauhaus designers used steel, concrete, and glass to create stark, geometric structures.

The Church, as well as the royal courts, provided employment to Germany's first professional musicians. Johann Sebastian Bach, a skilled church organist, developed a system of musical harmony that still dominates European music. Bach wrote hundreds of keyboard pieces as well as stirring religious works.

German composers of the nineteenth century were in the forefront of the Romantic movement. Ludwig van Beethoven's dramatic symphonies expanded the harmonic system first laid down by Bach. Robert Schumann and Felix Mendelssohn were known for their "program music," which was based on nonmusical ideas, characters, or stories. Schumann's wife, Clara, was a gifted composer and one of the finest concert pianists of her time.

Opera was the most important musical form to Richard Wagner, who drew on German legends and myths in his work. Wagner captivated audiences with *Tristan and Isolde* and *The Ring of the Nibelungen*, a cycle of four operas based on the *Nibelungenlied*.

Other styles of music also thrive in Germany. Berlin hosts an annual jazz festival, and rock bands like Interzone and Die Ärzte are internationally successful. Nina Hagen and Klaus Nomi have won fame for their punk rock performances.

Richard Wagner

Festivals and Food

Germans celebrate a variety of important dates on the calendar in a variety of unique and colorful ways. Many of these festivals are as different as the individual histories and cultures of the different German states and cities. The majority of German festivals mark events in the Christian year, including Christmas and Easter. As a prelude to Christmas Eve, Germans celebrate the Feast of Saint Nicholas on December 6, when good children find candy and nuts hidden in their shoes. (Misbehaving children receive nothing but a frightening visit from a stern costumed character named Ruprecht.) December 24 is the big day of gift giving, when Germans decorate the Tannenbaum (Christmas tree—a German creation) and open gifts. Following the opening of presents, German families gather for a feast of goose or turkey, before attending a midnight church service.

Perhaps the most famous German festival is Oktoberfest. This sixteen-day event has been held in Munich since 1810. Each year, more than 6 million people from around the world gather in the capital of Bavaria to drink beer, sing German songs, and enjoy German food. Many other German states and cities host a wide variety of festivals, both religious and secular, including horse festivals in northern Germany, wine festivals in western Germany, and an annual reenactment of the Pied Piper tale in the city of Hameln (formerly called Hamelin).

Each year, **Oktoberfest** draws millions of revelers to the Bavarian capital of Munich.

Germans eat large and hearty meals, and each region of the country boasts a food specialty. Bavarians enjoy Knödel, or filled dumplings. Cooks in Westphalia prepare cured and smoked ham with dark brown pumpernickel bread. Eel soup, herrings, oysters, and other seafood dishes are popular in the port city of Hamburg, which lies along the Elbe River. Traditional Christmas dinners throughout Germany include roast goose and stollen, a fruit bread. Adults drink beer or sweet white wine from the Rhine or Mosel valleys with their main courses.

Several traditional German dishes originated hundreds of years ago. Cooks created sauerkraut—cabbage soaked in brine—to preserve this common vegetable. They also ground up beef, pork, and veal into wurst, or sausages.

Beer (Bier in German) is the country's favorite drink. The average German drinks 36 gallons (138 liters) of it each year. Germany's breweries produce about 10 percent of the entire world's beer output, employing some 65,000 people. Although beer was invented thousands of years earlier, German monks are often credited with perfecting it during the Middle Ages.

POTATO SOUP

Potatoes are popular throughout Germany. This popular soup combines potatoes with chicken broth, carrots, and ham bone.

6 potatoes	1 ham bone
2 carrots	6 c. chicken broth
1 large onion	1 tsp. salt
1 medium parsnip	½ tsp. pepper
2 stalks celery	

1. Peel and cube potatoes. Peel and chop carrots, onions, and parsnip. Chop celery.
2. Place all ingredients in a large kettle. Bring to a boil over high heat. Reduce heat and simmer uncovered for 20 to 30 minutes, or until vegetables are tender.
3. Carefully pour soup into another pan through a large strainer. Remove ham bone.
4. With a large spoon, press vegetables through the sieve into soup. Stir well. Serve hot.

A German breakfast is usually light, with rolls and jam accompanied by coffee, tea, or milk. Germans traditionally eat a full meal at noon. This Mittagessen often begins with soup, followed by a meat course served with vegetables as well as noodles or dumplings. In recent times, however, the noon meal has become lighter, and many Germans have made the evening meal the largest of the day.

Sports and Recreation

While Germany was a divided nation, athletic clubs in both East and West Germany offered children, teenagers, and adults an opportunity for recreation and team sports. Millions of Germans still belong to at least one sports club, where they can compete with other sports enthusiasts.

Soccer (called Fussball in German) is the country's most popular sport. Cities, towns, and villages boast their own soccer teams. West Germany's national squad has won the World Cup soccer championship three times and the European championship twice. In 2002 the unified German team lost an exciting championship game to Brazil in the World Cup finals. Germans also compete in gymnastics, golf, horse riding, tennis, and other sports. Auto racing is also popular. German driver Michael Schumacher won his third straight Formula 1 World Championship—and fifth overall—in 2002.

After World War II, athletes from the former East Germany excelled in Olympic competition. The GDR regime implemented a system in which the best young athletes were groomed for Olympic competition. In 1992 all German Olympic athletes began competing as part of a unified team. At the 2000 Summer Olympic Games in Sydney, Australia, the German national team placed fifth in the medal count, winning fifty-six medals. German athletes won thirty-five medals at the 2002 Winter Olympics at Salt Lake City, Utah, the highest number of medals earned by any nation in a single winter Olympic games. Germans won gold in the men's team ski jump, women's biathlon relay, women's speedskating, women's single luge, men's double luge, and two-man bobsled.

Recreational sports in Germany include hiking, bicycling, and camping. Canoeists, rowers, sailors, and swimmers enjoy the country's many rivers and lakes. Downhill and cross-country skiing are the favorite winter sports in the Alps.

THE ECONOMY

After World War II, the U.S.-sponsored Marshall Plan brought about the rebuilding of West Germany. New industries in the region prospered, and, as a wide variety of consumer goods became available, the standard of living rapidly improved. This remarkable economic recovery is known as the Wirtschaftswunder, or "economic miracle." In East Germany, the postwar Communist government refused aid from the western democracies and took direct control of industries and agriculture. Although industrialization helped the region to recover from the war, shortages of food and consumer goods quickly developed. In the 1980s, the growing inefficiency of the system and the weakness of other Communist regimes in Eastern Europe led to the downfall of the East German government.

In the early 1990s, the unified German government took over the economy of East Germany. East German money was exchanged for West German currency, and generous social benefits were extended to the eastern population. An average of $65 billion has been transferred to the East from the West each year since reunification. Most

state-owned businesses were sold to private investors. Germany's economy boomed as easterners rushed to buy consumer goods. Construction in the East also helped to fuel the boom, employing nearly one-third of the workforce in the eastern states in the early 1990s.

In recent years, however, economic growth has slowed in both regions. The construction boom has faded, and unemployment is high throughout the country, especially in the eastern states, where it has hovered near 17 percent for the last several years. (The unemployment rate in the West, though lower, is still high at 8 percent.) German leaders' predictions that the East would catch up to the West within ten years of reunification have not come to pass. Another decade or more and many more billions in aid from the West will be required.

Manufacturing and Trade

The manufacturing sector drove Germany's recovery after World War II. West German companies expanded rapidly to meet the growing need for consumer goods, cars, textiles, and electrical equipment. Automaking boosted Germany's foreign trade, while the chemical, steel, and food-processing industries also produced exports. In 2000 the manufacturing sector provided 24 percent of the country's jobs.

The densely populated Ruhr valley in northwestern Germany has long been the country's principal industrial region. Extensive reserves of coal supply the Ruhr's huge steel plants, which turn out the raw material for construction of automobiles, ships, and machinery. Ruhr factories also produce chemicals, machinery, rubber, and textiles.

Workers in Berlin process food and beverages and make electrical goods and textiles. The shipyards of Bremerhaven, Kiel, and Hamburg construct oil tankers, fishing boats, cargo ships, and ferries. German industries also make clothing, furniture, scientific instruments, cameras, computers, toys, and leather goods. German aerospace companies work with several other European nations under the name Airbus to produce a line of popular passenger aircraft.

Although many eastern German companies have gone bankrupt, the region offers important advantages to firms from western Germany and

THE VOLKSWAGEN BEETLE

One of the world's most popular and distinctive cars, the VW Beetle was first developed in the 1930s. At the time, Adolf Hitler called on the German carmaker Volkswagen to build a car that would be cheap and efficient enough for most Germans to buy. With its rounded, buglike design, it was naturally given the name Beetle. Beetles were not produced in large numbers until after the war. Production skyrocketed in the 1950s and 1960s, however. The cars were particularly popular in America, where many families purchased them as second cars. Between 1945 and 1977, Volkswagen produced approximately 2 million Beetles. In recent decades, old Beetles have remained extremely popular, especially among young Americans. A new and completely redesigned model of the Beetle *(below)* was introduced in 1998.

Barges transport cargo up and down the Rhine, one of Europe's busiest rivers. Numerous canals connect the Rhine to other waterways in Germany, France, and the Netherlands.

from the rest of western Europe. Because the former Communist government tightly controlled prices and wages, production costs in the eastern zone have remained low. Several western German automakers have opened plants in eastern Germany, which has also attracted joint ventures with other European nations.

The postwar division of Germany created two separate economies with different trading links. East Germany exported its goods to other members of the Soviet bloc in Central and Eastern Europe.

Western Germany's rapid postwar growth eventually made it the largest exporter in Europe. The country's high standard of living and its strong demand for consumer goods have also created an important market for foreign importers. A reunified Germany sells more goods than it buys, giving the nation a trade surplus.

Germany is the world's second largest exporter, after the United States. The country exports vehicles, chemicals, optical instruments, electrical equipment, heavy machinery, and food. Major imports include energy products, clothing, textiles, food, and machinery. The country's most important trading partners include France, Italy, the Netherlands, the United States, Belgium, Luxembourg, the United Kingdom, Japan, Austria, and Switzerland.

Agriculture, Fishing, and Forestry

Since World War II, the number of farms in Germany has steadily decreased. Only 34 percent of the country's land remains under

Agriculture has played a smaller role in the German economy in the past century. Only a small percentage of German workers farm the land.

cultivation. German farms are small, averaging about 22 acres (9 hectares) in size. Many farmers work their land part-time and supplement their income with jobs in nearby cities and factories. Some large farms have joined cooperatives, in which workers pool their resources and share the profits from the sale of livestock and crops.

Vineyard

Crop and livestock production varies by region. Fruit orchards thrive in the Rhine River valley, while potatoes, grains, and fruit grow in the Thuringian Basin. Vineyards stretch along the banks of the Rhine, Mosel, and Neckar Rivers. Many farmers along the northern seacoast raise horses or dairy cattle. Beef cattle and sheep graze in the pastures of the Alpine foothills.

After World War II, East Germany organized its private farms into about 5,000 large, state-run cooperatives. In the early 1990s, the government of Germany ended these policies by selling acreages to individual farmers and turning the cooperatives into private companies. Nevertheless, many eastern German farmers cannot compete with the efficient, mechanized farms of western Germany. To help integrate German agriculture, the government provides financial support to newly privatized farms in the eastern zone.

Germany's fishing industry is centered on its North Sea ports, including Bremerhaven, one of the busiest fishing centers in Europe. The most important catches are herring, cod, sole, and flounder. German boats work in the North Sea, the Baltic Sea, and the North Atlantic Ocean near the coast of Greenland. Overfishing by Germany and by other European fleets, however, has depleted fish stocks in many of these areas.

Forests cover nearly one-third of Germany's land and provide about two-thirds of the country's lumber and paper products. Workers on government-controlled plantations carefully plan and monitor timber growth. Since 1975 the government has also required forestry companies to replant harvested areas. Despite these efforts at preservation, severe air pollution from German factories has damaged the country's forests. In recent decades, strict air pollution controls have brought about a drastic improvement in air quality that German officials believe will help the forests to recover.

Mining and Energy

Coal deposits near the Ruhr River became the mainstay of German industry during the 1800s. The Ruhr coalfields supplied fuel for merchant ships, steam locomotives, and steel factories. By the 1970s, mining companies had dug up much of the country's high-quality coal. Remaining reserves have proved expensive to extract, and coal is imported from other countries. Hard coal produces about 13 percent of the nation's energy. Other mineral deposits include lead, copper, tin, uranium, and zinc.

Eastern Germany's largest mineral resource is lignite coal. Found mainly in Saxony and in southern Brandenburg, lignite is used to

Lignite, or brown coal, is an important source of fuel for creating electricity. But the processing and burning of lignite has caused significant environmental problems.

generate electricity and as a raw material in the chemical industry. Lignite provides about 10 percent of the energy generated in Germany. The heavy smoke created by lignite burning led to serious environmental damage in East Germany, which lacked pollution-control equipment. Since reunification, the new eastern states have focused on reducing emissions, and factories and power plants have succeeded in reducing harmful emissions by more than half.

There are also small deposits of oil in the northern plains and in the Alpine Forelands, and energy companies have found natural gas beneath the floor of the North Sea. Nevertheless, high demand means Germany must import nearly all of its crude oil and most of its natural gas.

Germany is the world's leader in wind-generated power. More than 8,000 wind turbines are operating in the country, bringing power to more than 1.5 million households. Many of these wind farms are located in the northern regions of the country, and an offshore farm in the Baltic Sea became operational in 2000. The German government expects to double wind power production by 2010.

The German government is supporting the development of renewable energy sources, such as solar power and wind energy. The Renewable Energy Sources Act, passed in 2000, seeks to increase the proportion of energy created by renewable sources. In 2001 wind and solar power produced 7 percent of Germany's electricity. The government wants this percentage, already one of the highest in the world, to reach almost 13 percent by 2010. Long-term goals strive for half of all power to be produced by renewable sources by the middle of the century. At the same time, the German government is phasing out nuclear power. In 2001 the German government announced plans to shut down its 19 remaining nuclear power stations by 2020.

◉ Transportation and Tourism

The reunification of Germany and the elimination of closed borders in Eastern Europe have made the nation a key link in the European transportation network. Germany's rail system uses about 22,800 miles (36,700 km) of track. An urban train called the S-Bahn provides commuter service in the nation's largest cities. Many cities also have subway systems and bus networks.

The country's modern highways date to the 1930s, when the Nazi regime built a fast, four-lane roadway known as the Autobahn.

Germany's highway system, **the Autobahn,** has no official speed limit. Yet, in general, German traffic laws are strict and violations can result in the loss of driving privileges.

Autobahns, which make up a 6,900-mile (11,104-km) network, have no official speed limit.

Germany's merchant fleet includes more than 900 ships. Cargo ships and passenger ferries call at Hamburg, Bremen, Wilhelmshaven, and several other seaports. A canal links the Rhine, Main, and Danube Rivers, providing a route for river freight across Europe from the North Sea to the Black Sea.

Germany's largest airport, at Frankfurt, has become an important hub for European air traffic. Airports at Frankfurt and several other major cities handle both domestic and international flights. The nation's largest airline, Lufthansa, flies a modern fleet of passenger planes to destinations around the world.

The country's roads, ships, and planes bring in millions of traveling foreigners, who contribute more than $16 billion every year to Germany's economy. The capitals of Germany's former principalities attract visitors, who explore palaces, cathedrals, civic buildings, and castles. Even small villages boast historic churches and central market squares, where officials have taken care to preserve original street plans and architecture.

Tourists also seek natural attractions, such as the North Sea coast, the Harz Mountains, the Black Forest, and Lake Constance. Cruising boats follow the course of the Rhine River, where ruined castles loom

Germany's many sights, including its **beautiful lakes,** make the country a popular tourist destination.

over the valley's cliffs and hillsides. More than 80 special routes guide visitors away from major traffic arteries. The Romantic Road, for example, winds past Dinkelsbühl and other historic towns.

Many German cities host annual festivals. Every 10 years, visitors to the Bavarian village of Oberammergau can see a play that commemorates the village's survival of a deadly plague in 1632. During the 16 days of Oktoberfest in Munich, beer tents offer local brews as well as lively sideshows, musical performances, and bazaars. Since 1876 the Bavarian town of Bayreuth, where Richard Wagner lived and worked, has attracted thousands of people with performances of Wagnerian operas.

 Go to vgsbooks.com for up-to-date information about the German economy. You'll also find a link to a site with the current exchange rate where you can convert U.S. dollars to euros.

◉ The Future

Germany faces many of the same problems that confront its neighbors and partners in the European Union. As its population continues to decline, its large social welfare system will need significant changes in order to meet the population's needs. Yet, German citizens and the politicians who represent them have so far been reluctant to agree to the sacrifices required to make these changes. As in many other prosperous European nations, immigration has been a controversial topic.

While Germans are reluctant to embrace newcomers to their country, for fear of competition for jobs, their economy will be in need of such people and the labor they can provide in the future.

Meanwhile, Germany's economy continues to underperform. Experts place much of the blame for its sluggish growth on high taxes and a rigid labor market. Yet high taxes are needed to finance social welfare programs. Labor unions wield significant power, and they have made tremendous gains in ensuring good pay, benefits, and job security for their workers. From another perspective, however, the expense of compensating workers threatens to make German businesses uncompetitive in the world market. The tremendous expense of bringing the former East Germany into line with the western states has also caused a massive drain on the country's finances.

Yet, despite these difficulties, Germany still remains one of the world's great economic powers. With a skilled workforce and an excellent industrial infrastructure, Germany is sure to remain an economic leader for decades to come. While reunification has proven unexpectedly expensive, nearly all Germans agree it was the right course of action. With a long history—one often marred by war, devastation, and division—Germans can take pride in the way their country has become a peaceful, unified nation and a world leader.

Germans can look upon their rich past and feel hopeful for a strong future.

Timeline

c. 100,000 B.C.	Nomadic hunting groups migrate into what later became Germany.
c. 400 B.C.	Groups of Celts settle in the areas that would become southern and western Germany.
c. 100 B.C.	Teutons migrate from the north, pushing the Celts out of the area.
410	German Goths invade Italy and attack Rome.
476	Germanic soldiers serve in the Roman army. Odoacer, a Germanic leader, turns against the Romans, invades Rome, and declares himself ruler of Italy.
768	Charlemagne becomes ruler of the Franks and expands his empire to central and western Europe.
800	Pope Leo III crowns Charlemagne "Emperor of the Romans."
962	Otto I leads an army into Italy to fight for the pope. In return, Otto I is named Holy Roman Emperor. The Holy Roman Empire consists of hundreds of self-ruled territories.
1155	Frederick I ("Barbarossa") is named Holy Roman emperor. He adds parts of modern-day Poland and Hungary to his realm. Trade and industry increase.
1356	Holy Roman emperor Charles IV issues the Golden Bull, a set of laws that establishes a procedure for electing kings and provides a basic constitution for the empire.
1517	Martin Luther accuses the Roman Catholic Church of corruption.
1521	Luther is banned from the Catholic Church. Soon a Lutheran Church is formed and the Protestant Reformation sweeps across the northern German territories.
1555	War between Protestants and Catholics leads to the Peace of Augsburg. Each territory's ruler is allowed to choose between Catholicism and Lutheranism as the religion of their realm.
1618-1648	The Thirty Years' War begins as a conflict between the empire's Catholics and Protestants. In time the war spreads across the continent.
1756-1763	During the Seven Years' War, Frederick II of Prussia opposes Austria, Russia, France, Bavaria, and Saxony. Frederick's victories add territory to his realm.
1790s	After a popular revolution brings down the king of France, the German states and other European nations wage war with the French revolutionaries.

1806 French troops under the command of Napoleon Bonaparte invade and conquer parts of Germany.

1813 Prussian, Austrian, and Russian armies defeat Napoleon at the Battle of Leipzig.

1815 The Congress of Vienna reorganizes the German kingdoms into thirty-four states and four cities, called the German Confederation.

1870–1871 The Franco-Prussian War ends in defeat for France. The German states are united into a single nation-state, the German Empire.

1914–1918 World War I. Germany is defeated, and a revolution brings down the government in November 1918.

1919 Germany signs the Treaty of Versailles, requiring Germany to pay billions in war damages. A democratic government, the Weimar Republic, is established.

1920s The German economy is crippled by inflation and unemployment.

1933 Nazi Party leader Adolf Hitler is appointed chancellor.

1939–1945 World War II. Germany is defeated and divided into separate zones of occupation.

1949 The western German zones, occupied by British, French, and U.S. forces, become the Federal Republic of Germany (FRG). The Soviet-occupied eastern zones become the German Democratic Republic (GDR).

1955 The FRG joins the North Atlantic Treaty Organization. The GDR joins the Warsaw Pact.

1961 GDR authorities build the Berlin Wall to stop mass emigration to the West.

1973 Both the GDR and FRG are admitted to the United Nations.

1989 Economic problems lead to public protests in the GDR. Communist leader Erich Honecker is forced to resign. The GDR opens its border to the FRG. The Berlin Wall is torn down by German citizens.

1990 The two Germanys are reunited on October 3.

1999 The euro, the new European currency, begins to replace the German deutsche mark.

2001 The German government offers support to the United States after the September 11 terrorist attacks in New York City and Washington, D.C.

2002 Germany completes its currency changeover from the deutsche mark to the euro. German armed forces serve as peacekeepers in Afghanistan after the fall of Afghanistan's Taliban regime.

COUNTRY NAME Federal Republic of Germany

AREA 137,846 square miles (357,019 sq. km)

MAIN LANDFORMS North German Plain, Central Highlands, South German Hills, Alpine Forelands

HIGHEST POINT Zugspitze, 9,721 feet (2,963 m) above sea level

LOWEST POINT Freepsum Lake, 6.5 feet (2 m) below sea level

MAJOR RIVERS Danube, Elbe, Havel, Main, Mosel, Neckar, Oder, Regnitz, Rhine, Ruhr, Spree

ANIMALS Beavers, deer, grouse, lynx, ospreys, pine martens, sea eagles, wild boars

CAPITAL CITY Berlin

OTHER MAJOR CITIES Bremen, Cologne, Dresden, Düsseldorf, Frankfurt, Hamburg, Hannover, Leipzig, Munich

OFFICIAL LANGUAGE German

MONETARY UNIT Euro. 100 cents = 1 euro

GERMAN CURRENCY

The euro is the currency of the Federal Republic of Germany as well as eleven other European Union nations. The process of conversion from the German deutsche mark to the euro began in 1999, when the euro was first introduced. But the currency initially was used only for banking, credit card transactions, and other noncash purchases. Euro notes and coins were issued on January 1, 2002. All countries that have adopted the euro share the same bills. The fronts of euro coins share the same images, while each nation has created its own set of designs for the backs. All euro coins and bills are legal tender in every participating EU country.

The German federal flag, or Bundesflagge, consists of three equal horizontal stripes of black, red, and yellow. The colors date back to the Middle Ages, when Germany was part of the Holy Roman Empire. The colors reappeared during the Napoleonic Wars, when a group of army volunteers wore black uniforms with red braid and gold buttons. The flag was first adopted in 1848 by the short-lived Frankfurt Assembly. It did not become the official national flag until 1918. In 1933 Adolf Hitler abolished the flag, replacing it with the Nazi banner. The current flag was then reintroduced as the official banner of the Federal Republic of Germany in 1950.

The music to "Das Lied Der Deutschen," ("The Song of Germany") was composed by Austrian Franz Joseph Haydn in 1797. The lyrics were written by German poet August Heinrich Hoffmann von Fallersleben in 1841. The song first became the official national anthem in 1922 but was banned following World War II. In May 1952, it was reintroduced as the national anthem of the Federal Republic of Germany. Often only the third stanza is played at official events. Some Germans consider the first stanzas, which open with the words, "Germany, Germany over all" controversial, as they too strongly imply the nationalist sentiment that led the country into war in the 1900s.

"The Song of Germany" (third stanza)
Unity, Justice and Freedom
For the German Fatherland.
This is what we all must strive for,
Brotherly with heart and hand.
Unity, Justice and Freedom
Are the foundation for happiness.
Bloom in the radiance of this happiness,
Bloom, oh German Fatherland.

For a link to a site where you can listen to Germany's national anthem, "Das Lied Der Deutschen," go to vgsbooks.com.

JOHANN SEBASTIAN BACH (1685–1750) One of the most popular and prolific composers in history, Johann Sebastian Bach's huge number of works are performed throughout the world. Born in Eisenach, in Thuringia (central Germany), he studied music before joining an orchestra as a violinist when he was eighteen. He went on to serve as organist at a number of churches before being hired by a succession of German rulers. Throughout his life, Bach produced a massive volume of compositions, ranging from religious services for choirs to nonreligious orchestral works.

MARLENE DIETRICH (1901–1992) Known for her husky voice, shapely legs, and provocative sex appeal, Maria Magdelene Dietrich enjoyed a long career as one of the world's most recognizable movie stars. Born in Berlin, Dietrich appeared in several German silent films in the 1920s. In 1930 she received international attention for her role in the popular film, *The Blue Angel*. Moving to Hollywood, California, that same year, Dietrich went on to star in a series of highly successful American films, including *Morocco* (1930), *Shanghai Express* (1932), and *Destry Rides Again* (1939).

JOHANN WOLFGANG VON GOETHE (1749–1832) Considered Germany's greatest poet, Goethe was also a playwright, novelist, essayist, statesman, and scientist. Born in Frankfurt, he lived and studied in several European cities, including Leipzig, Strasbourg, and Weimar. Goethe's most famous work, the play *Faust*, tells the legend of Johann Faust, a man who makes a pact with the devil in order to gain knowledge and experience. (It was published in two parts in 1808 and 1832.) His other works include *Die Leiden des jungen Werthers, (The Sorrows of Young Werther)*, and *Italienische Reise (Italian Journey)*, a journal of his travels to Italy in the late 1780s.

STEFFI GRAF (b. 1969) One of the best tennis players of all time, Steffi Graf dominated her sport in the 1980s. Born in Mannheim and raised in Brühl, Graf's professional career began in 1982 at the age of thirteen. Within five years, she was the top-ranked player in the world. Her greatest year came in 1988, when she won the "grand slam" of tennis, winning the four major pro tournaments—the Australian Open, the French Open, Wimbledon, and the U.S. Open, while also winning a gold medal at the Summer Olympic Games in Seoul, South Korea.

JOHANNES GUTENBERG (1395?–1468?) As one of the earliest developers of the printing press and printing process, Gutenberg helped to make books more available throughout Europe. Born in Mainz to an aristocratic family, Gutenberg learned metalworking as a youth. With these skills, he developed the type mold, a piece of metal with a letter or character on it. These molds were then arranged to form lines and pages, which could be inked and pressed onto paper, creating a printed page. This printing process was far faster and cheaper than the older version of printing, which involved hand copying.

HELMUT KOHL (b. 1930) As chancellor of West Germany beginning in 1982, Kohl engineered the unification of the two Germanys in 1990. He led the unified Germany until 1998. Born in Ludwigshafen in western Germany, Kohl attended the University of Frankfurt and Heidelberg University, earning a doctorate in political science. He served in the parliament of the state of Rhineland-Palatinate from 1959 to 1976, serving as prime minister from 1969 to 1976. In 1976, he was elected to the Bundestag, where he served until he became chancellor. His Christian Democratic Union Party lost leadership of the government to Gerhard Schröder's Social Democratic Party in the 1998 elections.

KARL MARX (1818–1883) Philosopher, economist, journalist, and writer, Marx's writings on Socialism and Communism formed the basis of an economic and political revolution that transformed the world. Born in Trier, Prussia, Marx studied law and philosophy at Bonn University and the University of Berlin. Expelled from Prussia, and later France, for his radical views, Marx spent much of his life in London, where he worked as a journalist, organized a labor union, and wrote books on politics and economics. His two best-known works are *The Communist Manifesto* (co-written with Friedrich Engels) and *Das Kapital*, in which he predicts the downfall of capitalism and the rise of Communism.

KATARINA WITT (b. 1965) A world-champion figure skater, Katarina Witt won gold medals at the Winter Olympic Games in Sarajevo in 1984 and in Calgary in 1988. Born in Staaken in eastern Germany, she showed great promise as a figure skater at a young age. Accepted into a sports school—where she could study while dedicating herself to skating—Witt quickly became a top performer. She won the European Championship in 1983 and the World Championship in 1984. She went on to win the European Championship five more times and the World Championship three more times in the 1980s. Witt is also an actress who has appeared in a number of films and television programs.

CHRISTA WOLF (b. 1929) One of Germany's most popular authors, Christa Wolf creates works that often center on political themes. Born in Landsberg-Warthe, Wolf studied at the University of Leipzig and the University of Jena. A resident of East Germany following World War II, some of her works criticized the Communist regime, while others have focused on environmentalism, feminism, and Germans facing their Nazi past. In 1990 she published *Was bliebt (What Remains)*, an autobiographical account of the harassment she suffered at the hands of the Stasi, the East German secret police.

BERLIN Germany's capital and largest city is a popular destination for visitors. The city features a wide variety of architecture from every era of Germany's history. An island on the Spree River—where the city's first settlements appeared—is home to a variety of museums, as well as the Berlin Cathedral. The city's Kulturforum, or cultural center, includes a concert hall, a museum featuring musical instruments of past and present, a museum of arts and crafts, and an art library.

COLOGNE CATHEDRAL This magnificent cathedral dominates the skyline of Cologne. Every year, thousands of tourists come to marvel at its tall, ornamented spires and its treasury of golden religious objects. Each one of the church's arched doorways features dozens of intricately detailed figures. A long walk up winding steps to the top of one of the spires affords a breathtaking view of Cologne and the Rhine.

DRESDEN Despite having been almost completely destroyed by an Allied bombing raid in 1945, this city in eastern Germany is one of Europe's most attractive destinations. Decades of hard work by dedicated artisans have helped to restore the Saxony city's medieval glory. Dresden's most famous site is the Zwinger, a massive structure built in the early 1700s. Designed in the baroque style, its walls feature stunning statues. The Gemaldegalarie Alte Meister (Gallery of Old Masters) contains one of Europe's finest art collections, including works from Raphael, Rembrandt, and Vermeer.

MUNICH The capital of Bavaria is one of Germany's most beautiful cities and most popular tourist destinations. It features spectacular architecture from many different historical periods. These include the Neues Rathaus (New Town Hall), built in the Gothic style, with numerous statues and gables; and the Asamkirche, a church built in the Baroque style with colorful marble and ornate designs. Tourists and residents both walk the Marienplatz, a busy walkway lined with shops and restaurants, where street musicians often perform. The Deutsches Museum is one of the largest science and technology museums in the world. It features antique boats, trains, automobiles, printing presses, looms, and a large indoor historical aircraft collection.

NEUSCHWANSTEIN CASTLE This spectacular castle is set in the mountains of southern Bavaria, overlooking a beautiful lake (the Schwansee—Swan Lake) and waterfall. Built of pale gray granite, the multitowered structure reveals the eccentricities of its builder, Bavarian King Ludwig II. A lover of opera and a devoted patron to German composer Richard Wagner, Ludwig II had many of the castle's rooms painted with murals depicting scenes from Wagner's works. The king's apartments feature gilded woodwork, ornate furniture, and colorful murals. A special singing room was designed for musical performances, featuring scenes from Wagner's *Tannhäuser*.

capitalism: an economic system in which individuals control capital (money, goods, or the means of producing goods). In capitalist economies, availability and consumer demand determine prices of goods on the market.

chancellor: the chief minister of state in Germany

Communism: a political and economic model based on communal rather than private property. In a Communist system, goods and the means of producing these goods are controlled by the government and distributed according to need.

European Union: an organization of European countries that promotes cooperation among its members in matters of politics and economics

Gothic: the name given to a style of art and architecture of the later Middle Ages, generally from about the 1100s to 1400. Gothic architecture is highly decorative and features pointed arches and flying buttresses, a kind of support that allowed free space for stained glass windows. Many medieval German churches were built in the Gothic style.

gross domestic product (GDP): a measure of the total value of goods and services produced within a country in a certain amount of time (usually one year). A similar measurement is gross national product (GNP). GDP and GNP are often measured in terms of purchasing power parity (PPP). PPP converts values to international dollars, making it possible to compare how much similar goods and services cost to the residents of different countries.

Middle Ages: the period in western European history between ancient times and modern times, roughly from A.D. 400 to the 1500s. Society in the Middle Ages was dominated by agriculture and feudalism, a system in which a lord, prince, or other titled ruler owned land on which peasants worked.

nationalism: a philosophy or ideal valuing loyalty to one's own nation, preservation of national culture, and dedication to fulfilling the nation's needs

Protestantism: the general name for hundreds of non-Catholic Christian sects and denominations. First developed in Germany in the 1500s, Protestantism denies the universal authority of the pope, considers the Bible the only source of revealed truth, and regards faith in God's grace as one of its key principles.

reparations: the payment of damages; specifically, the compensation of money or materials paid by a defeated nation for damages and expenditures suffered by the victorious nation

Roman Catholicism: a branch of Christianity headed by the pope and based in Vatican City in Rome. Roman Catholicism is characterized by ceremony, ritual, and reverence for the Virgin Mary and saints as well as Jesus.

Socialism: a political and economic theory based on the ideal of social rather than individual control of goods and production. The ideals of socialism are very similar to those of Communism, but are generally broader and less extreme.

Selected Bibliography

BBC (British Broadcasting Corporation) News Online. 2002.
Website: < http://news.bbc.co.uk/2/hi/europe/default.stm>) (November 6, 2002)
The BBC's Europe section is an excellent resource for news on Germany and other European nations.

Bohnen, Agnes. *Women in Society: Germany*. New York: Marshall Cavendish, 1993.
This volume in the Women in Society series examines the roles of women in Germany throughout the country's long history. It also profiles the lives of a number of prominent German women.

Central Intelligence Agency (CIA). 2002.
Website: http://www.odci.gov/cia/publications/factbook/geos/gm.html (November 6, 2002)
The World Factbook section of the CIA's website contains basic information on Germany's geography, people, economy, government, communications, transportation, military, and transnational issues.

The Economist. 2002.
Website: <http://www.economist.com> (November 6, 2002)
Both the website and print edition of this British magazine provide excellent coverage of German economic and political news.

Egert-Romanowska, Joanna, Malgorzata Omilanowska, et al. *Germany*. New York: Dorling Kindersley Publishing, Inc., 2001.
Full of vivid photos and colorful illustrations, this volume in the DK Eyewitness Travel Guides series covers the hundreds of different sights throughout Germany. It also contains a brief introduction to German history and culture, as well as helpful information for visitors.

The Europa World Yearbook 2000. London: Europa Publications Limited, 2000.
This annual publication includes statistics on everything from agriculture and tourism to education and population density. It also contains a detailed account of Germany's history and current events, government, military, economy, social welfare, education, and a list of public holidays. Another survey explains details of the German government's structure, function, and Basic Law.

Fulbrook, Mary. *A Concise History of Germany*. New York: Cambridge University Press, 1990.
This book gives the reader a clear and informative guide to Germany's long and rich history.

Kitchen, Martin. *The Cambridge Illustrated History of Germany*. Cambridge, United Kingdom: Cambridge University Press, 1996.
This lavishly illustrated volume consists of a narrative history of Germany, from ancient Roman times to the present.

Population Reference Bureau. 2002.
Website: <http://www.prb.org> (November 6, 2002)
The annual statistics on this site provide a wealth of data on Germany's population, birth and death rates, fertility rate, infant mortality rate, and other useful demographic information.

Solsten, Eric., ed. *Germany: A Country Study.* **Washington, D.C.: Library of Congress, Federal Research Division, 1996.**
This volume from the Library of Congress's Area Handbook Series gives detailed information and analysis on Germany's history, society, social welfare, health care system, education system, environment, economy, government, foreign relations, and national security.

Byers, Ann. *The Holocaust Overview*. New York: Enslow Publishers, Inc., 1998.
The first volume of The Holocaust Remembered series traces anti-Semitism in Germany to its earliest origins. It follows the rise of the Nazi Party and its systematic plan for the elimination of the European Jewish population.

DW-World.de. **2002.**
Website: <http://dw-world.de/english>
This website, hosted by the German news service Deutsch-Welle, features current events, as well as features on German culture and lifestyle, science and technology, and business and economics.

The Economist.com—**Country Briefings.**
Website: <http://www.economist.com/countries/>
This section of *The Economist*'s website features fact sheets, news, economic data, economic forecasts, and explanations of the political forces and political structures of more than sixty countries, including Germany.

Facts about Germany. **2002.**
Website: <http://www.germany-info.org/relaunch/info/facts/facts.html>
The website for Germany's embassy in Washington, D.C., features a wide variety of facts and figures about the country's people, culture, economy, government, education system, and businesses.

Goethe, Johan Wolfgang von. *The Sorrows of Young Werther*. Translated by Elizabeth Mayer and Louise Brogan. New York: Vintage Books, 1990.
This is an excellent English translation of Goethe's famous story of passion, heartbreak, and suicide. This book, written as a series of letters, caused a sensation when it was first published in 1774.

Grey, Paul, and Rosemary Little. *Germany 1918–1945*. New York: Cambridge University Press, 1997.
This book covers the key events in German history during the tumultuous period that lasted from the end of World War I through the economic depression of the 1920s through the rise of the Nazi Party and the nation's defeat and destruction in World War II.

Keeley, Jennifer. *Life in the Hitler Youth*. San Diego, CA: Lucent Books, 2000.
This book reveals what life was like for young Germans who dedicated themselves to Adolf Hitler's Nazi regime in the 1930s and early 1940s. It thoughtfully explores the mindset of these young people and describes the important events of the time.

Mann, Thomas. *The Magic Mountain*. Translated by John E. Woods. New York: Vintage Books, 1996.
The Magic Mountain is the story of Hans Catorp, a young German who is forced to live in a sanatorium (clinic) in the Swiss Alps due to illness. While there, Hans is exposed to the many differing ideas and philosophies of prewar Europe.

Further Reading and Websites

McGowen, Tom. *Frederick the Great, Bismarck, and the Unification of Germany.* **New York: Enslow Publishers, Inc., 2002.**
Learn about the extensive and complicated process that ultimately united the many different states of Germany into one nation in the late 1800s.

Parnell, Helga. *Cooking the German Way.* **Minneapolis, MN: Lerner Publications Company, 2003.**
This volume from Lerner's Easy Menu Ethnic Cookbooks series features a history of Germany's cuisine, as well as several recipes of popular German dishes.

Reich, Susanna. *Clara Schumann: Piano Virtuoso.* **New York: Houghton Mifflin, 1999.**
This is a vivid and well-researched biography of Clara Schumann, the brilliant concert pianist and wife of Robert Schumann. It provides fascinating insights into the world of some of Germany's greatest musicians of the 1800s, as well as interesting details of the lives of German women during that time.

Schulz, Hagen. *Germany: A New History.* **Translated by Deborah Lucas Schneider. Cambridge, MA: Harvard University Press, 1998.**
This is an excellent history of Germany written by a professor from the Free University of Berlin.

Stein, R. Conrad. *Berlin.* **New York: Children's Press, 1997.**
This volume in the Cities of the World series profiles Germany's capital and largest city and features many photos.

vgsbooks.com.
Website: http://www.vgsbooks.com
Visit vgsbooks.com, the homepage of the Visual Geography Series®. You can get linked to all sorts of useful online information, including geographical, historical, demographic, cultural, and economic websites. The vgsbooks.com site is a great resource for late-breaking news and statistics.

Watts, Irene N. *Good-bye Marianne: A Story of Growing Up in Nazi Germany.* **Toronto, Ontario: Tundra Books, 1998.**
This is an autobiographical novel about growing up as a Jewish girl in Germany during the Nazi regime. Based on true events, the story follows a young German girl and her family as they experience increasing violence and hatred from the Nazis.

Wolf, Christa. *What Remains and Other Stories.* **Translated by Rick Takvorian and Heike Schwarzhauer. Chicago: University of Chicago Press, 1995.**
This is a collection of eight short stories written between 1960 and 1989. The title story describes her experience as a target of the Stasi, the East German secret police.

Zipes, Jack P., trans. *The Complete Fairy Tales of the Brothers Grimm.* **New York: Bantam Books, 1992.**
This colorful illustrated volume consists of a collection of famous German fairy tales by the Brothers Grimm, including "Hansel and Gretel," "Little Red Riding Hood," "Rumpelstiltskin," "Sleeping Beauty," "Cinderella," "Snow-White," and "Rapunzel."

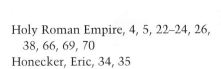

Captions for photos appearing on cover and chapter openers:

Cover: Constructed between the twelfth and the seventeenth centuries, Burg Eltz is one of Germany's finest medieval castles.

pp. 4–5 A group of houses known as the Ostzeile stand on one side of the Römerberg, the main square of Frankfurt am Main.

pp. 8–9 A castle overlooks rolling farmland near Bacharach, in Germany's Central Highlands region.

pp. 20–21 Odoacer, a Germanic leader, accepts the surrender of Roman emperor Romulus Augustulus in A.D. 476.

pp. 38–39 Germans young and old show support for their country.

pp. 46–47 The Berliner Dom is an imposing Protestant cathedral in the eastern part of Berlin.

pp. 56–57 The shipping industry in Hamburg has long made an important contribution to the German economy.

Photo Acknowledgments

The images in this book are used with the permission of: © A. A. M. Van der Heyden/Independent Picture Service, pp. 4–5, 8–9; Presentationmaps.com, pp. 6, 12; © Robert Fried/Robert Fried Photography/www.robertfriedphotography.com, pp. 10, 60 (top), 64; © TRIP/T. Bognar, pp. 11, 51, 53, 56–57; TRIP/R. Styles, p. 13; © Jost Schneider, p. 15; © Peter Turnley/CORBIS, pp. 16–17, 38–39; © TRIP/ TH-Foto Werbung, pp. 18, 19; © Bettmann/CORBIS, pp. 20–21, 48; Library of Congress, pp. 22 (LC-USZ62-9079), 24 (LC-USZC4-6894), 26 (LC-USZC2-4903), 29 (LC-USZ62-98186), 52 (bottom) (LC-USZ62-60978); National Archives, pp. 28 (NWDNS-111-B-2704), 31 (W & C #989), 32 (NWDNS-111-SC204322), 33 (NWDNS-286-ME-6 (2)); German Information Center, p. 35; © NETZHAUT/CORBIS SYGMA, p. 36; Action Press/ZUMA Press, p. 37; © HARTMUT SCHWARZBACH/Peter Arnold, p. 41 (top); © TRIP/M. Barlow, p. 41 (bottom); © TRIP/C. Garnham, p. 42; © Christel Gerstenberg/CORBIS, p. 44; © Murat Ayranci/Superstock, pp. 46–47; TV Times, p. 50; © TRIP/N. & J. Wiseman, p. 52 (top); © Todd Strand/Independent Picture Service, pp. 58, 68; © TRIP/B. Turner, pp. 59, 60 (bottom); © TRIP/M. O'Brien, p. 61; © Royalty-Free/CORBIS, p. 63; © Adam Jones, p. 65; Laura Westlund, p. 69.

Cover photo: © TRIP/N. & J. Wiseman. Back cover photo: NASA.